NWA:mo

k (144),
w (124)
... page 12 (123)

CONTENTS

From left to right: **Kasper Jacket** in Moss (103) and **Kasper Jacket in** Scarlet (140) pattern on page 82

INTRODUCTION

Carl Coat in Midnight (101)
pattern on page 48

Children should have fun – they should enjoy being mischievous and playful – in short they have a license to be Little Rascals. A mix of our signature, bright colours with more muted, elegant styles that still enable dressing up and play, Little Rascals is, we hope, a tribute to the essence of what being a child is all about.

COLOUR GIVES PERSONALITY

We remain devoted to the MillaMia ethos that you should be able to combine a love of knitting with a love of modern contemporary design and quality. We have also stayed true to the 17 colours that we launched our yarn range with. We may add more shades in the future but it is fun to see how versatile and rich these 17 colours can be when put in new designs and combinations. Some of the most interesting things happen when a pattern that is originally shown in a darker, core colour is reproduced in a brighter shade. Look at the Kasper Jacket as a great example of this – so practical and versatile in our dark shades, but in bright scarlet it practically shouts "notice me".

We think you can play with colour, so that it is not only an aesthetic decision but also takes into account personality. Put your wallflower in any of our brights and they will be noticed. Put a rough and tumble little one in one of our softer, light shades and see if you view and treat them differently. Colour is so powerful; we should all enjoy working with it.

Those who have knitted with MillaMia Naturally Soft Merino colours before will know that our goal was to create a set of shades that we felt would complement and enhance each other. As such don't be scared of experimenting with different colour combinations. So while we present options and alternative colour suggestions, why not try personalising your knitting by selecting your own variation of these? If you look at our website, www.millamia.com, you will find a 'Colour Tool' that allows you to experiment, 'playing' with different combinations and making your own colour design decisions.

HAND KNITTING CANNOT BE RIVALLED

The great thing about hand knitting is that the item you produce will be unique in some way, shape or form. Even with the most popular MillaMia designs from our previous collections it is always a thrill to see a new photo from a customer. Often you have been creative and tried out your own colour combinations, sometimes you have made your own design additions – an embellishment here or an alteration there. But even when they are knitted straight out of the book in the colourway shown, seeing them on a new child is always like seeing something fresh. The vagaries of hand knitting are part of its charm, and in some inexplicable way the love and care invested in producing a hand knit shines through – it creates a finished effect that truly money cannot buy.

We have always felt if you are investing the time it takes to make a hand knit, the end result should be a high quality item. Also you should work with materials that help you to enjoy the process. So we spent a lot of time with the mill developing our yarn to ensure that it is really great to work with – soft to touch, with a fabulous handle and that does not split as you are knitting. Many of our knitters are asked if the end result is machine knitted because of the even stitch definition. It feels great to be able to answer that, to the contrary, it is a hand knit. In truth the yarn does some of the work for you – the tight twist results in a really even, smooth stitch definition. It also means that the finished item is gorgeously soft for the children to wear – no risk of them crying "it's itchy" (the phrase all mothers dread!).

NEED SOME HELP?

We understand that sometimes even the most experienced knitter needs a bit of advice or help with a pattern, and of course beginners cannot be expected to know everything when they start out. At MillaMia we want to make knitting easy for you.

So whether it is a new technique you are struggling with or if you are a complete novice there are some marvellous resources available to you. The internet is fantastic – so many links and videos and tutorials at your fingertips.

If you need a starting point log on to our website www.millamia.com and search through the 'Making Knitting Easy' section. We provide advice and links, you can email us a question for our technical experts, organise a knitting class or find someone who can help knit the item for you. Not forgetting to look locally too, you should seek out any yarn shops or haberdashery departments. Many of these are staffed with real experts who will be able to help you. A full list of MillaMia stockists is available from our website – in these stores you will find people who are familiar and experienced with both the MillaMia yarns and patterns.

Finally, in our books do not forget to look at the Hints and Tips section for each pattern. We are constantly updating these in reprints. Based on our experience of customer queries we try to address concerns and questions upfront with these tips.

STILL STUCK?

We check every MillaMia pattern numerous times before we go to print and pride ourselves on having a good record to date with relatively few errata. Despite this, occasionally there can be errors in knitting patterns. If you see what you think is an error the best thing is to visit www.millamia.com where any errors that have been spotted will be published under 'Pattern Revisions'. If you cannot find the answer you are looking for, then do send an email (info@millamia.com) or contact us via the website and we will get back to you.

BASIC INFORMATION

SKILL LEVELS

Recognising that we are not all expert knitters we have graded each pattern in the book to allow you to gauge whether it is one that you feel confident to try. The grades are as follows:

Beginner: You have just picked up (or refound) knitting needles and are comfortable with the basic concepts of knitting. By reading carefully you can follow a pattern. Items such as scarves and blankets and simple jumpers are ideal for you to start with.

Beginner / Improving: Having knitted a few pieces you are now looking to try new things, for instance colour combinations and features such as pockets. You might surprise yourself by trying one of the simpler colourwork or cable patterns from our books – you will find that they are not as difficult as you may have thought. Bear in mind that most experienced knitters will be happy to help a beginner. Or look at our website for advice and help.

Improving: You have knitted a variety of items such as jumpers, cardigans and accessories in the past, and are comfortable with following patterns. You may have tried your hand at cable knitting and some form of colourwork before.

Experienced: You are comfortable with most knitting techniques. You have preferences and likes and dislikes, although are willing to try something new. You can read patterns quickly and are able to adapt them to your own requirements – for instance if resizing is needed.

YARN – SOME ADVICE

As there can be colour variations between dye lots when yarn is produced, we suggest that you buy all the yarn required for a project at the same time (with the same dye lot number) to ensure consistency of colour. The amount of yarn required for each pattern is based on average requirements meaning they are an approximate guide.

The designs in this book have been created specifically with a certain yarn composition in mind. The weight, quality, colours, comfort and finished knit effect of this yarn is ideally suited to these patterns. Substituting for another yarn may produce a garment that is different from the design and images in this book.

For the heavier items in our books we have used a technique where we 'use the yarn double'. This simply means using two balls of yarn at once on a thicker needle (in our patterns a 5mm (US 8) needle) to produce a thicker quality to the knitted fabric. An advantage of this technique is that the garment will be quicker to knit up.

TENSION / GAUGE

A standard tension is given for all the patterns in this book. As the patterns are in different stitch types (e.g. stocking, garter, rib, etc.) this tension may vary between patterns, and so you must check your tension against the recommendation at the start of the pattern. As matching the tension affects the final shape and size of the item you are knitting it can have a significant impact if it is not matched. Ensuring that you are knitting to the correct tension will result in the beautiful shape and lines of the original designs being achieved.

Micke Jumper
in Fuchsia (143)
pattern on page 42

To check your tension we suggest that you knit a square according to the tension note at the start of each pattern (casting on an additional 10 or more stitches to the figure given in the tension note and knitting 5 to 10 more rows than specified in the tension note). You should knit the tension square in the stitch given in the note (e.g. stocking, garter, moss, etc). Once knitted, mark out a 10cm by 10cm / 4in by 4in square using pins and count the number of stitches and rows contained within. If your tension does not quite match the one given try switching to either finer needles (if you have too few stitches in your square) or thicker needles (if you have too many stitches) until you reach the desired tension.

USEFUL RESOURCES

We believe that using quality trims with our knitwear gives the garments a professional finishing touch. Visit your local yarn/haberdashery shop for these items and MillaMia yarn, or visit www.millamia.com to order yarn directly or find local stockists.

SIZES

Alongside the patterns in this book we give measurements for the items – as two children of the same age can have very different measurements, this should be used as a guide when choosing which size to knit. The best way to ensure a good fit is to compare the actual garment measurements given in the pattern with the measurements of an existing garment that fits the child well.

Please note that where a chest measurement is given in the table at the top of each pattern this refers to the total measurement of the garment around the chest. When the cross chest measurement is given graphically in the accompanying diagrams this is half the around chest measurement. Children's clothes are designed with plenty of 'ease', this means that there is not as much shaping or fit to a child's garment as you will find in adult knitwear.

CARE OF YOUR GARMENT

See the ball band of MillaMia Naturally Soft Merino for washing and pressing instructions. Make sure you reshape your garments while they are wet after washing, and dry flat.

LANGUAGE

This book has been written in UK English. However, where possible US terminology has also been included and we have provided a translation of the most common knitting terms that differ between US and UK knitting conventions on page 9. In addition all sizes and measurements are given in both centimetres and inches throughout. Remember that when a knitting pattern refers to the left and right sides of an item it is referring to the left or right side as worn, rather than as you are looking at it.

READING COLOUR CHARTS

For some of the patterns in this book there are colour charts included. In a colour chart one square represents one stitch and one row. A key shows what each colour in the chart refers to. Remember that when following a knitting chart - unless specified otherwise in the note at the beginning of the pattern - right side rows (knit when working in stocking stitch) are worked from right to left, and wrong side rows (purl when working in stocking stitch) are worked from left to right.

The bottom row of the chart indicates the first row of knitting, and as you work your way up, each row of the chart illustrates the next row of knitting. Repeats are the same for all sizes, however different sizes will often require extra stitches as the repeat will not exactly fit. These stitches are marked by vertical lines showing the start and end of rows.

Mattias Cardigan in Midnight (101), Scarlet (140), Forget me not (120) and Seaside (161) pattern on page 68

ABBREVIATIONS

alt	alternate
approx	approximately
beg	begin(ning)
cont	continue
dec	decrease(ing)
foll	following
g-st	garter stitch
inc	increase(ing)
k or K	knit
k2 tog	knit two stitches together
m1	make one stitch by picking up the loop lying before the next stitch and knitting into back of it
m1p	make one stitch by picking up the loop lying before the next stitch and purling into back of it
mths	months
p or P	purl
p2 tog	purl two stitches together
patt	pattern
psso	pass slipped stitch over
pwise	purlwise
rib2 tog	rib two stitches together according to rib pattern being followed
rem	remain(ing)
rep	repeat(ing)
skpo	slip one, knit one, pass slipped stitch over – one stitch decreased
sl	slip stitch
st(s)	stitch(es)
st st	stocking stitch
tbl	through back of loop
tog	together
yf	yarn forward
yo	yarn over
yon	yarn over needle to make a st
yrn	yarn round needle
y2rn	wrap the yarn two times around needle. On the following row work into each loop separately working tbl into second loop
[]	work instructions within brackets as many times as directed

UK AND US KNITTING TRANSLATIONS

UK	US
Cast off	Bind off
Colour	Color
Grey	Gray
Join	Sew
Moss stitch	Seed stitch
Tension	Gauge
Stocking stitch	Stockinette stitch
Yarn forward	Yarn over
Yarn over needle	Yarn over
Yarn round needle	Yarn over
y2rn	yo2

KNITTING NEEDLE CONVERSION CHART

Metric, mm	US size
2	0
2.25	1
2.5	1
2.75	2
3	2
3.25	3
3.5	4
3.75	5
4	6
4.25	6
4.5	7
5	8
5.5	9
6	10
6.5	10.5
7	10.5
7.5	11
8	11
9	13
10	15

PIA
CARDIGAN

From left to right: **Pia Cardigan** in Grass (141), Daisy Yellow (142), Fuchsia (143), and Petal (122) and **Pia Cardigan** in Peacock (144), Lilac Blossom (123), Snow (124), and Daisy Yellow (142) pattern on page 12

PIA CARDIGAN

SKILL LEVEL **Improving**

SIZES / MEASUREMENTS

To fit age	1-2	2-3	3-4	4-5	years

ACTUAL GARMENT MEASUREMENTS

Chest	58	62	67	72	cm
	23	24 ½	26 ½	28 ½	in
Length to	28	32	36	40	cm
shoulder	11	12 ½	14 ¼	15 ¾	in
Sleeve	5	6	7	8	cm
length	2	2 ½	2 ¾	3 ¼	in

MATERIALS

3 (3:4:4) 50g/1 ¾oz balls of MillaMia Naturally Soft Merino in Peacock (144) (M).
One ball in each of Lilac Blossom (123), Daisy Yellow (142) and Snow (124).
Pair each of 3mm (US 2) and 3.25mm (US 3) knitting needles.
Circular 3mm (US 2) knitting needle.
5 buttons approx 15mm/½in in diameter.

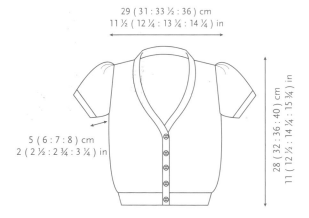

29 (31 : 33 ½ : 36) cm
11 ½ (12 ¼ : 13 ¼ : 14 ¼) in

5 (6 : 7 : 8) cm
2 (2 ½ : 2 ¾ : 3 ¼) in

28 (32 : 36 : 40) cm
11 (12 ½ : 14 ¼ : 15 ¾) in

TENSION / GAUGE

25 sts and 34 rows to 10cm/4in square over st st using 3.25mm (US 3) needles.

HINTS AND TIPS

The puff sleeves on this design are a real feature – so bear them in mind when you are sewing on the sleeves to the body. Also when working the back keeping a row count up to the armhole shaping will make it easier when knitting the front to determine where to start the front neck shaping.

ABBREVIATIONS

See page 9.

SUGGESTED ALTERNATIVE COLOURWAYS

Grass 141	Petal 122	Fuchsia 143	Daisy Yellow 142	Midnight 101	Plum 162	Seaside 161	Snow 124

NOTE

When working from Chart
Left front: right side rows are read from right to left starting at size indicated. Wrong side rows are read from left to right.
Right front: right side rows are read from left to right ending at size indicated. Wrong side rows are read from right to left.

BACK

With 3mm (US 2) needles and M cast on 74(80:86:92) sts.
1st rib row K2, [p1, k2] to end.
2nd rib row P2, [k1, p2] to end.
Rep the last 2 rows 7 times more.
Change to 3.25mm (US 3) needles.
Beg with a k row, cont in st st until back measures
16(19:22:25)cm/6 ¼(7 ½:8 ¾:9 ¾)in from cast on edge,
ending with a p row.
Shape armholes
Cast off 3(3:4:4) sts at beg of next 2 rows. 68(74:78:84) sts.
Next row K2, skpo, k to last 4 sts, k2 tog, k2.
Next row P to end.
Rep the last 2 rows 5(6:6:7) times. 56(60:64:68) sts.
Cont in st st until back measures 28(32:36:40)cm/11(12 ½:
14 ¼:15 ¾)in from cast on edge, ending with a p row.
Shape shoulders
Cast off 6(7:7:8) sts at beg of next 2 rows and 7(7:8:8) sts at
beg of foll 2 rows.
Leave rem 30(32:34:36) sts on a holder.

LEFT FRONT

With 3mm (US 2) needles and M cast on 33(36:39:42) sts.
1st rib row [K2, p1] to end.
2nd rib row [K1, p2] to end.
Rep the last 2 rows 7 times more.
Change to 3.25mm (US 3) needles.
Beg with a k row, cont in st st and patt from Chart until
16 rows less than back to armhole shaping have been worked,
ending with a p row.
Shape front neck
Next row Patt to last 2 sts, k2 tog.
Work 3 rows.
Rep the last 4 rows 3 times more.
Shape armhole and front neck
Next row Cast off 3(3:4:4) sts, patt to last 2 sts, k2 tog.

25(28:30:33) sts.
Next row Patt to end.
Next row Skpo, patt to end.
Next row Patt to end.
Next row Skpo, patt to last 2 sts, k2 tog.
Next row Patt to end.
Rep the last 4 rows 2(2:2:3) times.
2nd and 3rd sizes only
Next row Skpo, patt to end.
Next row Patt to end.
All sizes
16(18:20:21) sts.
Keeping armhole edge straight cont to dec at neck edge as set
on every 4th row until 13(14:15:16) sts rem.
Work straight until front matches back to shoulder, ending at
armhole edge.
Shape shoulder
Cast off 6(7:7:8) sts at beg of next row.
Work 1 row.
Cast off rem 7(7:8:8) sts.

RIGHT FRONT

With 3mm (US 2) needles and M cast on 33(36:39:42) sts.
1st rib row [P1, k2] to end.
2nd rib row [P2, k1] to end.
Rep the last 2 rows 7 times more.
Change to 3.25mm (US 3) needles.
Beg with a k row, cont in st st and patt from Chart until
16 rows less than back to armhole shaping have been worked,
ending with a p row.
Shape front neck
Next row Skpo, patt to end.
Work 3 rows.
Rep the last 4 rows 3 times more.
Shape armhole and front neck
Next row Skpo, patt to end.
Next row Cast off 3(3:4:4) sts, patt to end. 25(28:30:33) sts.

CHART rows 1-51

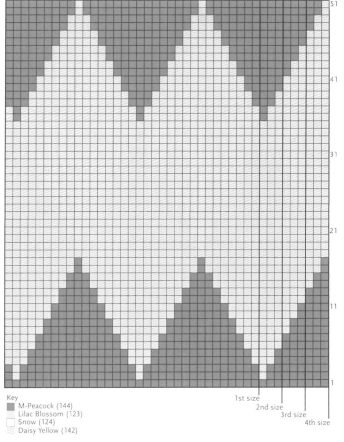

51
41
31
21
11
1

Key
- M-Peacock (144)
- Lilac Blossom (123)
- Snow (124)
- Daisy Yellow (142)

1st size
2nd size
3rd size
4th size

CHART rows 52 onwards

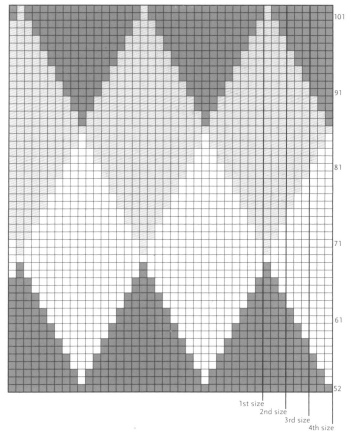

101
91
81
71
61
52

1st size
2nd size
3rd size
4th size

Next row Patt to last 2 sts, k2 tog.
Next row Patt to end.
Next row Skpo, patt to last 2 sts, k2 tog.
Next row Patt to end.
Rep the last 4 rows 2(2:2:3) times.
2nd and 3rd sizes only
Next row Patt to last 2 sts, k2 tog.
Next row Patt to end.
All sizes
16(18:20:21) sts.
Keeping armhole edge straight cont to dec at neck edge as set
on every 4th row until 13(14:15:16) sts rem.
Work straight until front matches back to shoulder, ending at
armhole edge.
Shape shoulder
Cast off 6(7:7:8) sts at beg of next row.
Work 1 row.
Cast off rem 7(7:8:8) sts.

SLEEVES

With 3mm (US 2) needles and M cast on 44(47:53:56) sts.
1st rib row K2, [p1, k2] to end.
2nd rib row P2, [k1, p2] to end.
Rep the last 2 rows twice more, and then the first row again.
Inc row Rib 4(3:6:6), m1, [rib 4, m1] 9(10:10:11) times, rib
4(4:7:6). 54(58:64:68) sts.
Change to 3.25mm (US 3) needles.
Beg with a k row cont in st st until sleeve measures 5(6:7:8)cm/
2(2 ½:2 ¾:3 ¼)in from cast on edge, ending with a p row.
Shape top
Cast off 3(3:4:4) sts at beg of next 2 rows. 48(52:56:60) sts.
Next row K2, skpo, k to last 4 sts, k2 tog, k2.
Next row P to end.
Rep the last 2 rows 6 times more. 34(38:42:46) sts.
Work 22(24:28:30) rows straight.
Next row K1, [k2 tog] 16(18:20:22) times, k1. 18(20:22:24) sts.
Next row P1, [p2 tog] 8(9:10:11) times, p1. 10(11:12:13) sts.
Cast off.

FRONT BAND

Join shoulder seams.
With right side facing, 3mm (US 2) circular needle and M,
pick up and k33(41:49:57) sts up right front edge, to beg of
neck shaping, 46(49:52:55) sts along right front neck edge,
k30(32:34:36) sts from back neck, pick up and k46(49:52:55) sts
down left front neck edge to beg of neck shaping,
33(41:49:57) sts along left front edge. 188(212:236:260) sts.
1st rib row P2, [k1, p2] to end.
This row sets the rib.
Rib 2 more rows.
Buttonhole row Rib 3, [work2 tog, yrn, rib 7(8:9:10)] 4 times,
work2 tog, yrn, rib to end.
Rib 3 more rows.
Cast off in rib.

TO MAKE UP

Join side and sleeve seams. Sew in sleeves, remembering the
puff sleeve nature of the design. Sew on buttons.

PETRA
WRAP
CARDIGAN
LISA
CABLE DRESS

From left to right: **Petra Wrap Cardigan** in Plum (162) pattern on page 20 and **Lisa Cable Dress** in Storm (102) pattern on page 24

19

PETRA WRAP CARDIGAN

SKILL LEVEL **Beginner / Improving**

SIZES / MEASUREMENTS

To fit age	1-2	2-3	3-4	4-5	years

ACTUAL GARMENT MEASUREMENTS

Chest	58	64	68	72	cm
	23	25	26 ¾	28 ½	in
Length	23	25	27	29	cm
	9	9 ¾	10 ½	11 ½	in
Sleeve	8	9	10	11	cm
length	3	3 ½	4	4 ½	in

MATERIALS

4(4:5:5) 50g/1 ¾oz balls of MillaMia Naturally Soft Merino in Snow (124).
Pair each of 3mm (US 2) and 3.25mm (US 3) knitting needles.
1 button approx 15mm/½in in diameter.

TENSION / GAUGE

25 sts and 34 rows to 10cm/4in square over st st using 3.25mm (US 3) needles.

HINTS AND TIPS

The perfect ballet wrap cardigan. So pretty. Take a careful look at the pictures to see how the waistband and tie are attached and also look at the photo on the previous page to see more details in the Plum coloured version. Remember that a button is also used on the inside of the waistband to secure the cardigan. The sleeves are puff sleeved so make sure you bear that in mind when sewing them in place.

ABBREVIATIONS

See page 9.

SUGGESTED ALTERNATIVE COLOURWAYS

Plum
162

Forget me not
120

Petal
122

Lilac Blossom
123

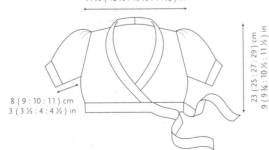

29 (32 : 34 : 36) cm
11 ½ (12 ½ : 13 ½ : 14 ¼) in

23 (25 : 27 : 29) cm
9 (9 ¾ : 10 ½ : 11 ½) in

8 (9 : 10 : 11) cm
3 (3 ½ : 4 : 4 ½) in

BACK

With 3.25mm (US 3) needles cast on 62(67:72:77) sts.
1st row K to end.
2nd row P to end.
3rd row (inc) K4, [m1, k5] to last 3 sts, m1, k3. 74(80:86:92) sts.
Beg with a p row, cont in st st until back measures 8(9:10:11)cm/
3(3 ½:4:4 ¼)in from cast on edge, ending with a p row.
Shape armholes
Cast off 4(5:6:7) sts at beg of next 2 rows. 66(70:74:78) sts.
Next row K2, skpo, k to last 4 sts, k2 tog, k2.
Next row P to end.
Rep the last 2 rows 6 times more. 52(56:60:64) sts.
Cont in st st until back measures 17(19:21:23)cm/
6 ¾(7 ½:8 ¼:9)in from cast on edge, ending with a p row.
Shape back neck
Next row K15(17:18:19), turn and work on these sts.
Dec one st at neck edge on next 4 rows. 11(13:14:15) sts.
Work 1 row.
Shape shoulder
Cast off 5(6:7:7) sts at the beg of next row.
Work 1 row.
Cast off rem 6(7:7:8) sts.
With right side facing return to rem sts, rejoin yarn and cast off
centre 22(22:24:26) sts, k to end.
Dec one st at neck edge on next 4 rows. 11(13:14:15) sts.
Work 2 rows.
Shape shoulder
Cast off 5(6:7:7) sts at the beg of next row.
Work 1 row.
Cast off rem 6(7:7:8) sts.

LEFT FRONT

With 3.25mm (US 3) needles cast on 54(57:61:64) sts.
1st row K to last 15 sts, p1, [k1, p1] 7 times.
2nd row K1, [p1, k1] 7 times, p to end.
These 2 rows set the st st with rib border.
3rd row (inc) K4(2:6:4), [m1, k5] to last 15 sts, m1, rib 15.
62(66:70:74) sts.
4th row Rib 15, p to end.
Dec row K to last 17 sts, k2 tog, rib 15.
Next row Rib 15, p to end.
Rep the last 2 rows until front measures the same as back to
armhole shaping, ending at side edge.
Shape armhole
Next row Cast off 4(5:6:7) sts, k to last 17 sts, k2 tog, rib 15.
Next row Rib 15, p to end.
Next row K2, skpo, k to last 17 sts, k2 tog, rib 15.
Next row Rib 15, p to end.
Rep the last 2 rows 6 times more.
Keeping armhole edge straight cont to dec at neck edge until
26(28:29:30) sts rem.
Work straight until front measures the same as back to
shoulder, ending at armhole edge.
Shape shoulder
Next row Cast off 5(6:7:7) sts, k to last 15 sts, rib 15.
Next row Rib 15, p to end.
Next row Cast off 6(7:7:8) sts, rib to end. 15 sts.
Cont in rib on these sts until band fits halfway round back neck.
Cast off in rib.

RIGHT FRONT

With 3.25mm (US 3) needles cast on 54(57:61:64) sts.
1st row P1, [k1, p1] 7 times, k to end.
2nd row P to last 15 sts, k1, [p1, k1] 7 times.
These 2 rows set the st st with rib border.
3rd row (inc) Rib 15, [m1, k5] to last 4(2:6:4) sts, m1, k4(2:6:4).
62(66:70:74) sts.

4th row P to last 15 sts, rib 15.

Dec row Rib 15, skpo, k to end.

Next row P to last 15 sts, rib 15.

Rep the last 2 rows until front measures the same as back to armhole shaping, ending at side edge.

Shape armhole

Next row Cast off 4(5:6:7) sts, p to last 15 sts, rib 15.

Next row Rib 15, skpo, k to last 4 sts, k2 tog, k2.

Next row P to last 15 sts, rib 15.

Rep the last 2 rows 6 times more.

Keeping armhole edge straight cont to dec at neck edge until 26(28:29:30) sts rem.

Work straight until front measures the same as back to shoulder, ending at armhole edge.

Shape shoulder

Next row Cast off 5(6:7:7) sts, p to last 15 sts, rib 15.

Next row Rib 15, k to end.

Next row Cast off 6(7:7:8) sts, rib to end. 15 sts.

Cont in rib on these sts until band fits halfway round back neck.

Cast off in rib.

SLEEVES

With 3mm (US 2) needles cast on 56(62:68:74) sts.

Rib row [K1, p1] to end.

Rep the last row 15 times more.

Change to 3.25mm (US 3) needles.

Cont in st st until sleeve measures 8(9:10:11)cm/3(3 ½:4:4 ½)in from cast on edge, ending with a p row.

Shape top

Cast off 4(5:6:7) sts at beg of next 2 rows. 48(52:56:60) sts.

Next row K2, skpo, k to last 4 sts, k2 tog, k2.

Next row P to end.

Rep the last 2 rows 6 times more. 34(38:42:46) sts.

Work 22(24:28:30) rows straight.

Next row K1, [k2 tog] 16(18:20:22) times, k1. 18(20:22:24) sts.

Next row P1, [p2 tog] 8(9:10:11) times, p1. 10(11:12:13) sts.

Cast off.

WAISTBAND AND TIE

With 3mm (US 2) needles cast on 15 sts.

1st rib row K2, [p1, k1] to last 3 sts, p1, k2.

2nd rib row K1, [p1, k1] to end.

These 2 rows form the rib.

Work a further 2 rows.

Buttonhole row Rib 6, p2 tog, y2rn, k2 tog, rib 5.

Next row Rib to end, working twice into y2rn.

Cont in rib until band fits around waist starting at left front edge and finishing at right front edge.

Work a further 50cm/19 ¾in.

Cast off in rib.

TIE

With 3mm (US 2) needles cast on 15 sts.

1st rib row K2, [p1, k1] to last 3 sts, p1, k2.

2nd rib row K1, [p1, k1] to end.

These 2 rows form the rib.

Cont in rib until tie measures 50cm/19 ¾in.

Cast off in rib.

TO MAKE UP

Join shoulder seams. Join cast off edges of back neckband and sew to back neck edge. Join side and sleeve seams. Sew in sleeves. Sew on waistband to cast on edges of back and fronts. Sew tie to left front at side seam. Sew button on inside of right front to match buttonhole.

LISA CABLE DRESS

SKILL LEVEL Experienced

SIZES / MEASUREMENTS

To fit age	1-2	2-3	3-4	4-5	5-6	6-7	years

ACTUAL GARMENT MEASUREMENTS

Chest	52	56	60	66	70	76	cm
	20 ½	22	23 ½	26	27 ½	30	in
Length to	45	50	55	60	65	70	cm
back neck	17 ¾	19 ¾	21 ¾	23 ¾	25 ½	27 ½	in
Sleeve	5	5	6	6	7	7	cm
length	2	2	2 ½	2 ½	3	3	in

MATERIALS

5(6:6:7:8:9) 50g/1¾oz balls of MillaMia Naturally Soft Merino in Storm (102).
Pair each of 3mm (US 2) and 3.25mm (US 3) knitting needles.
Circular 3mm (US 2) and 3.25mm (US 3) knitting needles.
Cable needle.
4 buttons approx 15mm/½in in diameter.

TENSION / GAUGE

25 sts and 34 rows to 10cm/4in square over st st using 3.25mm (US 3) needles.

HINTS AND TIPS

This stunning dress will look fabulous on little girls. Nice and warming it is great for the colder months. Pay attention as you set the cable pattern and then you can relax and enjoy the rest of the work. When working the collar on the circular needles remember you are working back and forth – not in the round.

ABBREVIATIONS

C10F, cable 10 forward - slip next 5 sts on a cable needle and hold at front of work, k5, then k5 from cable needle.
C4F, cable 4 front - slip next 2 sts on a cable needle and hold at front of work, k2, then k2 from cable needle.
See also page 9.

SUGGESTED ALTERNATIVE COLOURWAYS

Putty Grey 121   Scarlet 140   Plum 162   Snow 124

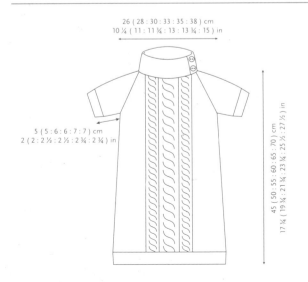

26 (28 : 30 : 33 : 35 : 38) cm
10 ¼ (11 : 11 ¾ : 13 : 13 ¾ : 15) in

5 (5 : 6 : 6 : 7 : 7) cm
2 (2 : 2 ½ : 2 ½ : 2 ¾ : 2 ¾) in

45 (50 : 55 : 60 : 65 : 70) cm
17 ¾ (19 ¾ : 21 ¾ : 23 ¾ : 25 ½ : 27 ½) in

BACK

With 3mm (US 2) needles cast on 72(82:92:102:112:122) sts.
1st rib row P2, [k3, p2] to end.
2nd rib row K2, [p3, k2] to end.
Rep the last 2 rows 7 times more.
Change to 3.25mm (US 3) needles.
Beg with a k row cont in st st.
Work 24(18:16:14:14:14) rows.
Dec row K4, skpo, k to last 6 sts, k2 tog, k4.
Work 23(17:15:13:11:9) rows.
Rep the last 24(18:16:14:12:10) rows 1(3:5:7:9:11) times more, and then the dec row again.
66(72:78:84:90:96) sts.
Cont in st st until back measures 33(37:41:45:49:53)cm/13(14 ½: 16 ¼:17 ¾:19 ¼:21)in from cast on edge, ending with a p row.
Shape raglan armholes
Cast off 4 sts at beg of next 2 rows. 58(64:70:76:82:88) sts.
Next row K1, skpo, k to last 3 sts, k2 tog, k1.
Next row P to end.
Next row K to end.
Next row P to end.
Rep the last 4 rows 4 times more. 48(54:60:66:72:78) sts.
Next row K1, skpo, k to last 3 sts, k2 tog, k1.
Next row P to end.
Rep the last 2 rows 8(10:12:14:16:18) times more.
30(32:34:36:38:40) sts.
Leave these sts on a spare needle.

FRONT

With 3mm (US 2) needles cast on 72(82:92:102:112:122) sts.
1st rib row P2, [k3, p2] to end.
2nd rib row K2, [p3, k2] to end.
Rep the last 2 rows 6 times more, and then the first row again.
Inc row Rib 23(28:33:38:43:48), m1, rib 12, m1, rib 2, m1, rib 12, m1, rib 23(28:33:38:43:48). 76(86:96:106:116:126) sts.

Change to 3.25mm (US 3) needles.
1st row K20(25:30:35:40:45), p2, k4, p2, k3, p2, k10, p2, k3, p2, k4, p2, k20(25:30:35:40:45).
2nd row P to end.
3rd and 4th rows As 1st and 2nd rows.
5th row K20(25:30:35:40:45), p2, C4F, p2, k3, p2, C10F, p2, k3, p2, C4F, p2, k20(25:30:35:40:45).
6th row As 2nd row.
7th to 10th rows Rep 1st and 2nd rows twice.
11th row K20(25:30:35:40:45), p2, C4F, p2, k3, p2, k10, p2, k3, p2, C4F, p2, k20(25:30:35:40:45).
12th row As 2nd row.
These 12 rows form the patt and are repeated.
Work 12(6:4:2:2:2) rows in patt.
Dec row K4, skpo, patt to last 6 sts, k2 tog, k4.
Work 23(17:15:13:11:9) rows in patt.
Rep the last 24(18:16:14:12:10) rows 1(3:5:7:9:11) times more, and then the dec row again.
70(76:82:88:94:100) sts.
Cont in patt until front measures 33(37:41:45:49:53)cm/13(14 ½: 16 ¼:17 ¾:19 ¼:21)in from cast on edge, ending with a p row.
Shape raglan armholes
Cast off 4 sts at beg of next 2 rows. 62(68:74:80:86:92) sts.
Next row K1, skpo, patt to last 3 sts, k2 tog, k1.
Next row P to end.
Next row Patt to end.
Next row P to end.
Rep the last 4 rows 4 times more. 52(58:64:70:76:82) sts.
Next row K1, skpo, patt to last 3 sts, k2 tog, k1.
Next row P to end.
Rep the last 2 rows 7(9:11:13:15:17) times more, and then the dec row again. 34(36:38:40:42:44) sts.
Next row P to end, dec one st over each small cable and 2 sts over centre cable. 30(32:34:36:38:40) sts.
Leave these sts on a holder.

SLEEVES

With 3mm (US 2) needles cast on 52(62:62:72:72:82) sts.
1st rib row P2, [k3, p2] to end.
2nd rib row K2, [p3, k2] to end.
Rep the last 2 rows 2(2:3:3:4:4) times more, and then the first row again.
Inc row Rib 25(30:30:35:35:40), m1, rib 2, m1, rib 25(30:30:35: 35:40). 54(64:64:74:74:84) sts.
Change to 3.25mm (US 3) needles.
1st row K20(25:25:30:30:35), p2, k10, p2, k20(25:25:30:30:35).
2nd row P to end.
3rd and 4th rows As 1st and 2nd rows.
5th row K20(25:25:30:30:35), p2, C10F, p2, k20(25:25:30:30:35).
6th row As 2nd row.
7th to 12th rows Rep 1st and 2nd rows 3 times.
These 12 rows form the patt and are repeated.
Cont in patt until sleeve measures 5(5:6:6:7:7)cm/2(2:2 ½: 2 ½:2 ¾:2 ¾)in from cast on edge, ending with a p row.
Shape raglan sleeve top
Cast off 4 sts at beg of next 2 rows. 46(56:56:66:66:76) sts.
Next row K2, skpo, patt to last 4 sts, k2 tog, k2.
Next row P to end.
Next row Patt to end.
Next row P to end.
Rep the last 4 rows 2(0:2:0:2:0) times.
Next row K2, skpo, patt to last 4 sts, k2 tog, k2.
Next row P to end.
Rep the last 2 rows until 14(16:16:18:18:20) sts rem, ending with a p row.
Leave these sts on a holder.

COLLAR

Slip first 10(11:11:12:12:13) sts of left sleeve onto a spare needle, using 3.25mm (US 3) circular needle cast on 6 sts, k next 3(4:4:5:5:6) sts from left sleeve, k last st tog with first st on front, k28(30:32:34:36:38), k last st tog with first st on right sleeve, k12(14:14:16:16:18), k last st tog with first st on back, inc 4(6:2:4:0:2) sts evenly across 28(30:32:34:36:38)sts, k last st tog with first st on left sleeve from spare needle, k9(10:10:11:11:12) from spare needle. 94(104:104:114:114:124) sts.
Work backwards and forwards in rows.
1st row (right side of collar) K6, [p2, k3] to last 8 sts, p2, k6.
2nd row K1, p5, [k2, p3] to last 8 sts, k2, p5, k1.
These 2 rows form the rib.
Work a further 4 rows.
Buttonhole row Rib to last 6 sts, k2 tog, y2rn, skpo, k2.
Rib 9(9:9:11:11:11) rows.
Rep the last 10(10:10:12:12:12) rows twice more, and then the buttonhole row again.
Rib 5 rows.
Cast off loosely in rib.

TO MAKE UP

Join raglan seams. Join side and sleeve seams. Sew on buttons.

LUDO BLANKET

SKILL LEVEL Improving

SIZES / MEASUREMENTS
Size   One size

ACTUAL MEASUREMENTS
56cm/22in by 63cm/25in

MATERIALS
Seven 50g/1 ¾oz balls of MillaMia Naturally Soft Merino in Snow (124).
Pair of 3.25mm (US 3) knitting needles.
Cable needle.

TENSION / GAUGE
25 sts and 34 rows to 10cm/4in square over st st using 3.25mm (US 3) needles.

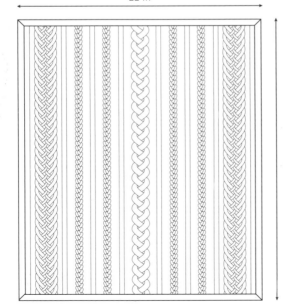

56 cm
22 in

63 cm
25 in

HINTS AND TIPS
This elegant, timeless cable blanket is made in several panels and then sewn together. This makes it easier to manage while knitting and also makes it a more solid, constructed piece once finished. If you wanted to make the blanket bigger you could of course simply add more panels on either side and / or work the panels to a longer length. Be sure to block the panels nice and flat before you join them together and we advise using mattress stitch to sew the pieces together for a neat finish.

ABBREVIATIONS
Cr12L, cross 12 left - [k6, turn, p6, turn] twice, k6, slip these 6 sts on a cable needle and hold at front of work, k next 6 sts from left hand needle.
Cr12R, cross 12 right - k12, [turn, p6, turn, k6] twice, slip these 6 sts on a cable needle and hold at front of work.
C4B, cable 4 back - slip next 2 sts on a cable needle and hold at back of work, k2, then k2 from cable needle.
C4F, cable 4 front - slip next 2 sts on a cable needle and hold at front of work, k2, then k2 from cable needle.
C9B, cable 9 back - slip next 5 sts on a cable needle and hold at back of work, k4, slip p st from cable needle onto left hand needle, p1, then k4 from cable needle.
C9F, cable 9 front - slip next 5 sts on a cable needle and hold at front of work, k4, slip p st from cable needle onto left hand needle, p1, then k4 from cable needle.
See also page 9.

SUGGESTED ALTERNATIVE COLOURWAYS

Plum
162

Fawn
160

Forget me not
120

Petal
122

PIPPI (centre panel)

Using 3.25mm (US 3) needles cast on 26 sts.
1st row K3, p4, k12, p4, k3.
2nd row P3, k4, p12, k4, p3.
3rd row K3, p4, k1, [m1, k2] 5 times, m1, k1, p4, k3. 32 sts.
4th row P3, k4, p18, k4, p3.
Cont in patt.
5th row K3, p4, Cr12R, k6, p4, k3.
6th row P3, k4, p12, p6 from cable needle, k4, p3.
7th row K3, p4, k18, p4, k3.
8th row P3, k4, p18, k4, p3.
9th row K3, p4, k6, Cr12L, p4, k3.
10th row P3, k4, p6 from cable needle, p12, k4, p3.
11th row K3, p4, k18, p4, k3.
12th row P3, k4, p18, k4, p3.
5th to 12th rows form the patt and are repeated.
Cont in patt until panel measures 61cm/24in from cast on edge, ending with a 6th or 10th row.
Next row K3, p4, [k1, k2 tog] 6 times, p4, k3. 26 sts.
Next row P3, k4, p12, k4, p3.
Leave these sts on a holder.

GARLIC BRAID (make 2)

Using 3.25mm (US 3) needles cast on 38 sts.
1st row K3, p4, k6, p4, k4, p4, k6, p4, k3.
2nd row P3, k4, p6, k4, p4, k4, p6, k4, p3.
3rd row K3, p4, k2, [m1, k2] twice, p4, k4, p4, k2, [m1, k2] twice, p4, k3. 42 sts.
4th row P3, k4, p8, k4, p4, k4, p8, k4, p3.
Cont in patt.
5th row K3, p4, [C4B] twice, p4, k4, p4, [C4B] twice, p4, k3.
6th row P3, k4, p8, k4, p4, k4, p8, k4, p3.
7th row K3, p4, k2, C4F, k2, p4, k4, p4, k2, C4F, k2, p4, k3.
8th row P3, k4, p8, k4, p4, k4, p8, k4, p3.
5th to 8th rows form the patt and are repeated.

Cont in patt until panel measures 61cm/24in from cast on edge, ending with a 5th or 7th row.
Next row P3, k4, p2, [p2 tog] twice, p2, k4, p4, k4, p2, [p2 tog] twice, p2, k4, p3. 38 sts.
Next row K3, p4, k6, p4, k4, p4, k6, p4, k3.
Next row P3, k4, p6, k4, p4, k4, p6, k4, p3.
Leave these sts on a holder.

DOUBLE FANTASY (right hand side)

Using 3.25mm (US 3) needles cast on 34 sts.
1st row K5, p4, k18, p4, k3.
2nd row P3, k4, p18, k4, p5.
3rd row K5, p4, k1, [m1, k3] 5 times, m1, k2, p4, k3. 40 sts.
4th row P3, k4, [p4, k1] 4 times, p4, k4, p5.
Cont in patt.
5th row K5, p4, k4, [p1, C9F] twice, p4, k3.
6th row P3, k4, [p4, k1] 4 times, p4, k4, p5.
7th row K5, p4, [k4, p1] 4 times, k4, p4, k3.
8th row P3, k4, [p4, k1] 4 times, p4, k4, p5.
9th row K5, p4, [C9B, p1] twice, k4, p4, k3.
10th row P3, k4, [p4, k1] 4 times, p4, k4, p5.
11th to 16th rows Rep 7th and 8th rows 3 times.
5th to 16th rows form the patt and are repeated.
Cont in patt until panel measures 61cm/24in from cast on edge, ending with a 5th or 9th row.
Next row P3, k4, p1, [p2 tog, p2] 5 times, p2 tog, p1, k4, p5. 34 sts.
Next row K5, p4, k18, p4, k3.
Next row P3, k4, p18, k4, p5.
Leave these sts on a holder.

DOUBLE FANTASY (left hand side)

Using 3.25mm (US 3) needles cast on 34 sts.
1st row K3, p4, k18, p4, k5.
2nd row P5, k4, p18, k4, p3.
3rd row K3, p4, k1, [m1, k3] 5 times, m1, k2, p4, k5. 40 sts.
4th row P5, k4, [p4, k1] 4 times, p4, k4, p3.

Cont in patt.

5th row K3, p4, k4, [p1, C9F] twice, p4, k5.

6th row P5, k4, [p4, k1] 4 times, p4, k4, p3.

7th row K3, p4, [k4, p1] 4 times, k4, p4, k5.

8th row P5, k4, [p4, k1] 4 times, p4, k4, p3.

9th row K3, p4, [C9B, p1] twice, k4, p4, k5.

10th row P5, k4, [p4, k1] 4 times, p4, k4, p3.

11th to 16th rows Rep 7th and 8th rows 3 times.

5th to 16th rows form the patt and are repeated.

Cont in patt until panel measures 61cm/24in from cast on edge, ending with a 5th or 9th row.

Next row P5, k4, p1, [p2 tog, p2] 5 times, p2 tog, p1, k4, p3. 34 sts.

Next row K3, p4, k18, p4, k5.

Next row P5, k4, p18, k4, p3.

Leave these sts on a holder.

TOP EDGING

Join panels together, with Pippi panel in the centre, the Double Fantasy panels on the outer edges and Garlic Braids in between.

With right side facing, using 3.25mm (US 3) needles, k33 from Double Fantasy holder, k2 tog (the last st from Double Fantasy and first st from Garlic Braid), k36 from Garlic Braid holder, k2 tog (the last st from Garlic Braid and first st from Pippi panel), k24 from Pippi panel holder, k2 tog (the last st from Pippi panel and the first st from the second Garlic Braid panel), k36 from second Garlic Braid holder, k2 tog (the last st from second Garlic Braid panel and first st from second Double Fantasy panel), k33 from second Double Fantasy holder. 166 sts.

✳✳1st row K to end.

2nd row K2, m1, k to last 2 sts, m1, k2.

Rep the last 2 rows once more.

Cast off ✳✳.

BOTTOM EDGING

With right side facing, using 3.25mm (US 3) needles, pick up and k166 sts along cast on edges.

Work as given for top edging from ✳✳ to ✳✳.

SIDE EDGING (do twice – one for each side)

With right side facing, using 3.25mm (US 3) needles, pick up and k175 sts along side edges.

Work as given for top edging from ✳✳ to ✳✳.

MAKE UP

Join corners of edgings.

MAGNUM
CARDIGAN

From left to right: **Magnum Cardigan** in Claret (104),
Magnum Cardigan in Forget me not (120) and
Magnum Cardigan in Fawn (160) pattern on page 34

MAGNUM CARDIGAN

SKILL LEVEL Experienced

SIZES / MEASUREMENTS

To fit age	1-2	2-3	3-4	4-5	5-6	6-7	years

ACTUAL GARMENT MEASUREMENTS

Chest	66	71	76	81	86	91	cm
	26	28	30	32	34	36	in
Length to	31	34	37	40	43	46	cm
shoulder	12 ¼	13 ½	14 ½	15 ¾	17	18	in
Sleeve	19	22	25	28	31	34	cm
length	7 ½	8 ¼	10	11	12 ¼	13 ½	in

MATERIALS

6(7:8:9:11:12) 50g/1 ¾oz balls of MillaMia Naturally Soft Merino in Fawn (160).
Pair each of 2.75mm (US 2) and 3.25mm (US 3) knitting needles.
2.75mm (US 2) circular knitting needle.
Cable needle.
8 buttons approx15mm/½in in diameter.

TENSION / GAUGE

25 sts and 34 rows to 10cm/4in square over st st using 3.25mm (US 3) needles.
32 sts and 34 rows to 10cm/4in square over patt using 3.25mm (US 3) needles.

HINTS AND TIPS

This pattern is a treat for cable lovers who will relish working in the pattern on all pieces. Try to block the ribbing on the front bands nice and wide by wet blocking the item so that the rib does not pull back too much from the bottom edges.

ABBREVIATIONS

Cable 6 forward, C6F - slip next 3 sts onto cable needle and hold at front of work, k3, then k3 from cable needle.
Cable 12 forward, C12F - slip next 6 sts onto cable needle and hold at front of work, k6, then k6 from cable needle.
See also page 9.

SUGGESTED ALTERNATIVE COLOURWAYS

Forget me not
120

Claret
104

Seaside
161

Snow
124

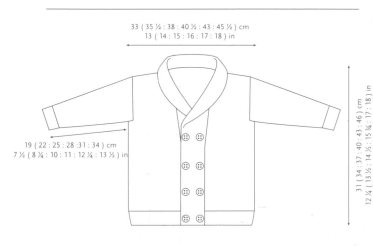

33 (35 ½ : 38 : 40 ½ : 43 : 45 ½) cm
13 (14 : 15 : 16 : 17 : 18) in

19 (22 : 25 : 28 :31 : 34) cm
7 ½ (8 ¼ : 10 : 11 : 12 ¼ : 13 ½) in

31 (34 : 37 : 40 : 43 : 46) cm
12 ¼ (13 ½ : 14 ½ : 15 ¾ : 17 : 18) in

BACK

With 2.75mm (US 2) needles cast on 102(110:118:126:134:142) sts.

1st row (right side) P2, [k2, p2] to end.

2nd row K2, [p2, k2] to end.

Rep the last 2 rows 4 times more, and then the first row again.

Inc row (wrong side) Rib 32(36:40:44:48:52), [m1, rib 6, m1, rib 10] twice, m1, rib 6, m1, rib 32(36:40:44:48:52). 108(116:124:132:140:148) sts.

Change to 3.25mm (US 3) needles.

Work in patt as follows:

1st row [P2, k2] 0(1:2:3:4:5) times, [p2, k2, p2, k6] twice, [p2, k2, p2, k12] 3 times, [p2, k2, p2, k6] twice, p2, [k2, p2] 1(2:3:4:5:6) times.

2nd and every wrong side row P to end.

3rd row As 1st row.

5th row [P2, k2] 0(1:2:3:4:5) times, [p2, k2, p2, C6F] twice, [p2, k2, p2, k12] 3 times, [p2, k2, p2, C6F] twice, p2, [k2, p2] 1(2:3:4:5:6) times.

7th and 9th rows As 1st row.

11th row [P2, k2] 0(1:2:3:4:5) times, [p2, k2, p2, C6F] twice, [p2, k2, p2, C12F] 3 times, [p2, k2, p2, C6F] twice, p2, [k2, p2] 1(2:3:4:5:6) times.

12th row P to end.

These 12 rows form the patt and are repeated.

Cont in patt until back measures 19(21:23:25:27:29)cm/7 ½ (8 ¼:9:9 ¾:10 ½:11 ½)in from cast on edge, ending with a wrong side row.

Shape armholes

Cast off 5 sts at beg of next 2 rows. 98(106:114:122:130:138) sts.

Cont in patt until back measures 31(34:37:40:43:46)cm/12 ¼ (13 ½:14 ½:15 ¾:17:18)in from cast on edge, ending with a wrong side row.

Shape shoulders

Next row Cast off 15(16:17:18:19:20) sts at beg of next 4 rows. 38(42:46:50:54:58) sts.

Cast off in patt.

LEFT FRONT

With 2.75mm (US 2) needles cast on 41(45:49:53:57:61) sts.

1st row (right side) P2, [k2, p2] to last 3 sts, k3.

2nd row P3, k2, [p2, k2] to end.

Rep the last 2 rows 4 times more, and then the first row again.

Inc row (wrong side) Rib 7, m1, rib 6, m1, rib 28(32:36:40:44:48). 43(47:51:55:59:63) sts.

Change to 3.25mm (US 3) needles.

Work in patt as follows:

1st row [P2, k2] 0(1:2:3:4:5) times, [p2, k2, p2, k6] twice, p2, k2, p2, k12, p1.

2nd and every wrong side row P to end.

3rd row As 1st row.

5th row [P2, k2] 0(1:2:3:4:5) times, [p2, k2, p2, C6F] twice, p2, k2, p2, k12, p1.

7th and 9th rows As 1st row.

11th row [P2, k2] 0(1:2:3:4:5) times, [p2, k2, p2, C6F] twice, p2, k2, p2, C12F, p1.

12th row P to end.

These 12 rows form the patt and are repeated.

Cont in patt until front measures 19(21:23:25:27:29)cm/7 ½ (8 ¼:9:9 ¾:10 ½:11 ½)in from cast on edge, ending with a wrong side row.

Shape armhole and front neck

Next row Cast off 5 sts, patt to last 2 sts, k2 tog. 37(41:45:49:53:57) sts.

Keeping armhole edge straight dec one st at neck edge on every foll 4th(4th:3rd:3rd:3rd:3rd) row until 30(32:34:36:38:40) sts rem.

Work straight until front measures the same as back to shoulder, ending at armhole edge.

Shape shoulder

Next row Cast off 15(16:17:18:19:20) sts, patt to end.

Work 1 row.

Cast off rem 15(16:17:18:19:20) sts.

RIGHT FRONT

With 2.75mm (US 2) needles cast on 41(45:49:53:57:61) sts.
1st row (right side) K3, p2, [k2, p2] to end.
2nd row K2, [p2, k2] to last 3 sts, p3.
Rep the last 2 rows 4 times more, and then the first row again.
Inc row (wrong side) Rib 28(32:36:40:44:48), m1, rib 6, m1, rib 7. 43(47:51:55:59:63) sts.
Change to 3.25mm (US 3) needles.
Work in patt as follows:
1st row P1, k12, [p2, k2, p2, k6] twice, p2, [k2, p2] 1(2:3:4:5:6) times.
2nd and every wrong side row P to end.
3rd row As 1st row.
5th row P1, k12, [p2, k2, p2, C6F] twice, p2, [k2, p2] 1(2:3:4:5:6) times.
7th and 9th rows As 1st row.
11th row P1, C12F, [p2, k2, p2, C6F] twice, p2, [k2, p2] 1(2:3:4:5:6) times.
12th row P to end.
These 12 rows form the patt and are repeated.
Cont in patt until front measures 19(21:23:25:27:29)cm/7 ½ (8 ¼:9:9 ¾:10 ½:11 ½)in from cast on edge, ending with a wrong side row.
Shape armhole and front neck
Next row Skpo, patt to end.
Next row Cast off 5 sts, patt to end. 37(41:45:49:53:57) sts.
Keeping armhole edge straight dec one st at neck edge on every foll 4th(4th:3rd:3rd:3rd:3rd) row until 30(32:34:36:58:40) sts rem.
Work straight until front measures the same as back to shoulder, ending at armhole edge.
Shape shoulder
Next row Cast off 15(16:17:18:19:20) sts, patt to end.
Work 1 row.
Cast off rem 15(16:17:18:19:20) sts.

SLEEVES

With 2.75mm (US 2) needles cast on 50(50:58:58:66:66) sts.
1st row (right side) K2, [p2, k2] to end.
2nd row P2, [k2, p2] to end.
Rep the last 2 rows 3 times more, and then the first row again.
Inc row (wrong side) Rib 22(22:26:26:30:30), m1, rib 6, m1, rib 22(22:26:26:30:30). 52(52:60:60:68:68) sts.
Change to 3.25mm (US 3) needles.
Work in patt as follows:
1st row [K2, p2] 2(2:3:3:4:4) times, k6, p2, k2, p2, k12, p2, k2, p2, k6, [p2, k2] 2(2:3:3:4:4) times.
2nd and every wrong side row P to end.
3rd row As 1st row.
5th row [K2, p2] 2(2:3:3:4:4) times, C6F, p2, k2, p2, k12, p2, k2, p2, C6F, [p2, k2] 2(2:3:3:4:4) times.
7th and 9th rows As 1st row.
11th row [K2, p2] 2(2:3:3:4:4) times, C6F, p2, k2, p2, C12F, p2, k2, p2, C6F, [p2, k2] 2(2:3:34:4) times.
12th row P to end.
These 12 rows set the patt and are repeated.
Inc and work into patt one st at each end of the next row and every foll 3rd row until there are 76(82:92:98:106:112) sts.
Cont straight until sleeve measures 19(22:25:28:31:34)cm/ 7 ½(8 ¾:9 ¾:11:12 ¼:13 ½)in from cast on edge, ending with a wrong side row.
Mark each end of last row with a coloured thread.
Work a further 6 rows.
Cast off.

LEFT FRONT BAND AND COLLAR

With 2.75mm (US 2) circular needle, cast on
29(31:33:35:37:39) sts, with right side facing, pick up
and k39(43:47:51:55:59) sts from shoulder to beg of
neck shaping, 54(60:66:72:78:84) sts to cast on edge.
122(134:146:158:170:182) sts.
1st row P2, [k2, p2] to end.
This row sets the rib.
Next 2 rows Rib 28(30:32:34:36:38), turn, rib to end.
Next 2 rows Rib 32(34:36:38:40:42), turn, rib to end.
Next 2 rows Rib 36(38:40:42:44:46), turn, rib to end.
Cont in this way for a further 16(16:18:18:20:20) rows work 4
more sts on every alt row.
Work 3 rows across all sts.
Buttonhole row Rib 4, yf, rib2 tog, [rib 12(14:16:18:20:22), yf,
rib2 tog] 3 times, rib to end.
Rib a further 13 rows.
Buttonhole row Rib 4, yf, rib2 tog, [rib 12(14:16:18:20:22),
rib2 tog] 3 times, rib to end.
Rib a further 3 rows.
Cast off in rib.

RIGHT FRONT BAND AND COLLAR

With 2.75mm (US 2) circular needle and right side facing,
pick up and k54(60:66:72:78:84) sts to beg of neck shaping,
39(43:47:51:55:59) sts to shoulder, cast on 29(31:33:35:37:39) sts.
122(134:146:158:170:182) sts.
Working in rib as given for left front band and collar, work as
folls:
1st row P2, [K2, p2] to end.
This row sets the rib.
Work 1 more row.
Next 2 rows Rib 28(30:32:34:36:38), turn, rib to end.
Next 2 rows Rib 32(34:36:38:40:42), turn, rib to end.
Next 2 rows Rib 36(38:40:42:44:46), turn, rib to end.
Cont in this way for a further 16(16:18:18:20:20) rows work 4
more sts on every alt row.
Work 20 rows across all sts.
Cast off in rib.

MAKE UP

Join shoulder seams. Join collar seam. Sew collar to back
neck edge. Join side and sleeve seams, joining final rows after
markers to cast off sts underarm. Sew in sleeves. Sew on
buttons.

MICKE
JUMPER

From left to right:
Micke Jumper in Fuchsia (143),
Micke Jumper in Grass (141) and
Micke Jumper in Midnight (101)
pattern on page 42

MICKE JUMPER

SKILL LEVEL **Beginner / Improving**

SIZES / MEASUREMENTS

To fit age	1-2	2-3	3-4	4-5	5-6	6-7	years

ACTUAL GARMENT MEASUREMENTS

Chest	58	64	70	76	84	90	cm
	23	25	27 ½	30	33	35 ½	in
Length to	30	32	34	36	38	40	cm
shoulder	11 ¾	12 ½	13 ½	14 ¼	15	15 ¾	in
Sleeve	19	22	25	28	31	34	cm
length	7 ½	8 ½	9 ¾	11	12 ¼	13 ½	in

MATERIALS

5(5:6:7:7:8) 50g/1 ¾oz balls of MillaMia Naturally Soft Merino in Fuchsia (143).
Pair each of 2.75mm (US 2) and 3.25mm (US 3) needles.
Circular 3.25mm (US 3) knitting needle.

TENSION / GAUGE

25 sts and 34 rows to 10cm/4in square over st st using 3.25mm (US 3) needles.

HINTS AND TIPS

This batwing jumper is on-trend and comfortable. Also a surprisingly easy knit. Just remember to fold the collar over and block in place to get the asymmetric, diagonal line that is so essential to the look of this item. The circular needle is used as there are too many stitches at some points to work on regular knitting needles. You are still knitting back and forth in rows for this pattern, not in the round.

SUGGESTED ALTERNATIVE COLOURWAYS

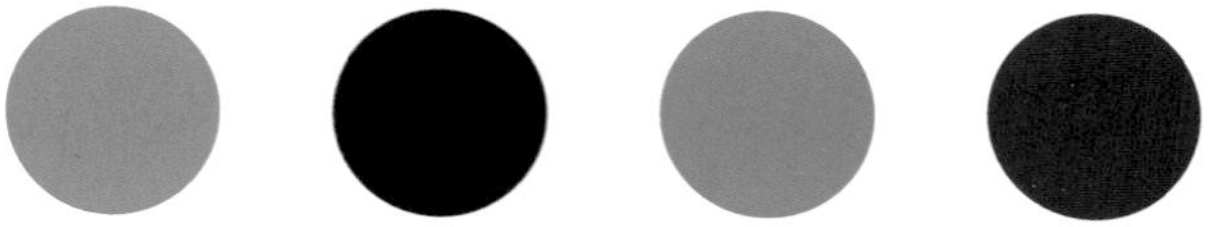

Grass	Midnight	Peacock	Scarlet
141	101	144	140

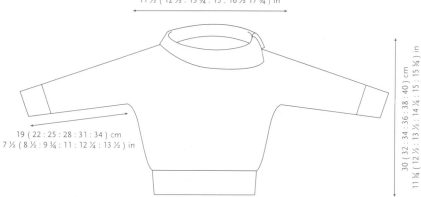

29 (32 : 35 : 38 : 42 : 45) cm
11 ½ (12 ½ : 13 ¾ : 15 : 16 ½ 17 ¾) in

19 (22 : 25 : 28 : 31 : 34) cm
7 ½ (8 ½ : 9 ¾ : 11 : 12 ¼ : 13 ½) in

30 (32 : 34 : 36 : 38 : 40) cm
11 ¾ (12 ½ : 13 ½ : 14 ¼ : 15 : 15 ¾) in

BACK AND FRONT ALIKE

With 2.75mm (US 2) needles cast on 74(82:90:98:106:114) sts.
1st row [K1, p1] to end.
This row forms the rib.
Work a further 27 rows.
Change to 3.25mm (US 3) needles.
Beg with a k row cont in st st until work measures
18(19:20:21:22:23)cm/7(7 ½:8:8 ¼:8 ¾:9)in from cast on edge,
ending with a p row.
Change to 3.25mm (US 3) circular needle, and cont working
back and forth in rows.
Shape sleeves
Cast on 6(7:8:9:10:11) sts at beg of next 12 rows.
146(166:186:206:226:246) sts.
Cont straight until work measures 26(28:30:32:34:36)cm/10 ¼
(11:11 ¾:12 ½:13 ½:14)in from cast on edge, ending with a p row.
Shape neck
Next row K55(63:71:79:87:95), turn and work on these sts for
first side of neck.
Next row P to end.
Shape upper sleeves
Next row Cast off 7(8:9:10:11:12), k to last 3 sts, k2 tog, k1.
Next row P to end.
Rep the last 2 rows 4 times more. 15(18:21:24:27:30) sts.
Shape shoulder
Next row Cast off 7(9:10:12:13:15) sts, k to end.
Next row P to end.
Cast off rem 8(9:11:12:14:15) sts.
With right side facing slip centre 36(40:44:48:52:56) sts on a
holder, rejoin yarn to rem sts, k to end.
Next row P to end.
Shape upper sleeves
Next row K1, skpo, k to end.
Next row Cast off 7(8:9:10:11:12) sts, p to end.
Rep the last 2 rows 4 times more. 15(18:21:24:27:30) sts.
Shape shoulder
Next row K to end.

Next row Cast off 7(9:10:12:13:15) sts, p to end.
Next row K to end.
Cast off rem 8(9:11:12:14:15) sts.

NECKBAND

Join right shoulder and upper sleeve seam.
With right side facing and 3.25mm (US 3) needles, pick up
and k12 sts down left side of front neck, 36(40:44:48:52:56) sts
from holder, pick up and k12 sts up right side of front neck,
12 sts down right side of back neck, 36(40:44:48:52:56) sts
from holder, pick up and k12 sts up left side of back neck.
120(128:136:144:152:160)sts.
1st row [K1, p1] to end.
This row forms the rib.
Work a further 25(27:29:31:33:35) rows.
Cast off in rib.

CUFFS

Join left shoulder and upper sleeve seam.
With right side facing and 3.25mm (US 3) needles, pick up and
k50(54:62:66:70:74) sts along row ends of sleeves.
1st row [K1, p1] to end.
This row forms the rib.
Work a further 15(17:19:21:23:25) rows.
Cast off in rib.

MAKE UP

Join cuff, under arm and side seams.

CARL COAT JESPER JUMPER JESSI SCARF

From left to right:
Carl Coat in Midnight (101) pattern on page 48,
Jesper Jumper in Midnight (101), Grass (141),
and Snow (124) pattern on page 52 and
Jessi Scarf in Scarlet (140) pattern on page 58

CARL COAT

SKILL LEVEL Beginner / Improving

SIZES / MEASUREMENTS

To fit age	1-2	2-3	3-4	4-5	years

ACTUAL GARMENT MEASUREMENTS

Chest	71	75	80	84	cm
	28	29 ½	31 ½	33	in
Length to	33	37	41	45	cm
shoulder	13	14 ½	16	17 ¾	in
Sleeve	22	24	27	30	cm
length	8 ¾	9 ½	10 ½	11 ¾	in

MATERIALS

9(10:12:13) 50g/1 ¾oz balls of MillaMia Naturally Soft Merino in Midnight (101) (M).
Pair each of 4.50mm (US 7) and 5mm (US 8) knitting needles.
6 large buttons approx 21mm/⅞ in in diameter.

TENSION / GAUGE

18 sts and 26 rows to 10cm/4in square over st st using 5mm (US 8) needles and yarn double.

HINTS AND TIPS

Time for the boys to also get an outercoat. Using the yarn double makes this coat lovely and warm with a nice structured fabric. Try to keep the two balls of yarn that you are working with on different levels to avoid the threads tangling.

ABBREVIATIONS

See page 9.

SUGGESTED ALTERNATIVE COLOURWAYS

Grass	Seaside	Storm	Moss
141	161	102	103

NOTE

Use yarn double **throughout**.

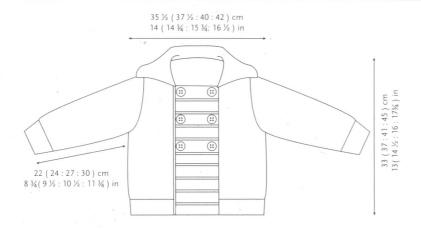

35 ½ (37 ½ : 40 : 42) cm
14 (14 ¾ : 15 ¾: 16 ½) in

22 (24 : 27 : 30) cm
8 ¾(9 ½ : 10 ½ : 11 ¾) in

33 (37 : 41 : 45) cm
13(14 ½ : 16 : 17¾) in

49

BACK

With 4.50mm (US 7) needles and yarn used double cast on 68(68:74:74) sts.

1st rib row P2, [k4, p2] to end.

2nd rib row K2, [p4, k2] to end.

Rep the last 2 rows twice more, dec(inc:-:inc) 2(2:0:4) sts evenly across last row. 66(70:74:78) sts.

Change to 5mm (US 8) needles.

Beg with a k row cont in st st until back measures 19(22:25:28)cm/ 7 ½(8 ½:9 ¾:11)in from cast on edge, ending with a p row.

Shape armholes

Cast off 4 sts at beg of next 2 rows. 58(62:66:70) sts.

Next row K2, skpo, k to last 4 sts, k2 tog, k2.

Next row P to end.

Rep the last 2 rows 2(3:3:4) times more. 52(54:58:60) sts.

Work straight until armhole measures 14(15:16:17)cm/5 ½(6: 6 ¼:6 ¾)in, ending with a wrong side row.

Shape shoulders

Cast off 6(6:7:7) sts at beg of next 2 rows and 7(7:8:8) sts at beg of foll 2 rows.

Cast off rem 26(28:28:30) sts.

LEFT FRONT

With 4.50mm (US 7) needles and yarn used double cast on 25(25:31:31) sts.

1st rib row [P2, k4] to last st, p1.

2nd rib row K1, [p4, k2] to end.

Rep the last 2 rows twice more, -(inc:dec:-) 0(2:2:0) sts evenly across last row. 25(27:29:31) sts.

Change to 5mm (US 8) needles.

Beg with a k row cont in st st until front measures 19(22:25:28)cm/ 7 ½(8 ½:9 ¾:11)in from cast on edge, ending with a p row.

Shape armhole

Next row Cast off 4 sts, k to end. 21(23:25:27) sts.

Next row P to end.

Next row K2, skpo, k to end.

Next row P to end.

Rep the last 2 rows 2(3:3:4) times more. 18(19:21:22) sts.

Work straight until armhole measures 9(10:10:11)cm/ 3 ½(4:4:4 ½)in, ending with a wrong side row.

Shape neck

Next row K to last 4 sts, k2 tog, k2.

Next row P to end.

Rep the last 2 rows 4(5:5:6) times more. 13(13:15:15) sts.

Work straight until front measures same as back to shoulder, ending at armhole edge.

Shape shoulder

Cast off 6(6:7:7) sts at beg of next row.

Work 1 row.

Cast off rem 7(7:8:8) sts.

RIGHT FRONT

With 4.50mm (US 7) needles and yarn used double cast on 25(25:31:31) sts.

1st rib row P1, [k4, p2] to end.

2nd rib row [K2, p4] to last st, k1.

Rep the last 2 rows twice more, -(inc:dec:-) 0(2:2:0) sts evenly across last row. 25(27:29:31) sts.

Change to 5mm (US 8) needles.

Beg with a k row cont in st st until front measures 19(22:25:28)cm/ 7 ½(8 ½:9 ¾:11)in from cast on edge, ending with a k row.

Shape armhole

Next row Cast off 4 sts, p to end. 21(23:25:27) sts.

Next row K to last 4 sts, k2 tog, k2.

Next row P to end.

Rep the last 2 rows 2(3:3:4) times more. 18(19:21:22) sts.

Work straight until armhole measures 9(10:10:11)cm/ 3 ½ (4:4:4 ½)in, ending with a wrong side row.

Shape neck

Next row K2, skpo, k to end.

Next row P to end.

Rep the last 2 rows 4(5:5:6) times more. 13(13:15:15) sts.

Work straight until front measures same as back to shoulder,

ending at armhole edge.
Shape shoulder
Cast off 6(6:7:7) sts at beg of next row.
Work 1 row.
Cast off rem 7(7:8:8) sts.

SLEEVES

With 4.50mm (US 7) needles and yarn used double cast on
32(32:38:38) sts.
1st rib row P2, [k4, p2] to end.
2nd rib row K2, [p4, k2] to end.
Rep the last 2 rows 4 times more, dec(inc:-:inc) 2(2:0:4) sts
evenly across last row. 30(34:38:42) sts.
Change to 5mm (US 8) needles.
Beg with a k row cont in st st.
Work 2(4:4:6) rows.
Inc row K3, m1, k to last 3 sts, m1, k3.
Work 3 rows.
Rep the last 4 rows 8(8:9:9) times more, and then the inc row
again. 50(54:60:64) sts.
Cont straight until sleeve measures 22(24:27:30)cm/8 ¾(9 ½:
10 ½:11 ¾)in from cast on edge, ending with a p row.
Shape sleeve top
Cast off 4 sts at beg of next 2 rows. 42(46:52:56) sts.
Next row K2, skpo, k to last 4 sts, k2 tog, k2.
Next row P to end.
Rep the last 2 rows 4(5:5:6) times more. 32(34:40:42) sts.
Cast off 3 sts at beg of next 6(6:8:8) rows. 14(16:16:18) sts.
Cast off.

BUTTONBAND

With right side facing, starting at cast on edge, using
4.50mm (US 7) needles and yarn used double, pick up and
k58(66:70:78) sts evenly up right front edge.
1st rib row P2, [k2, p2] to end.
2nd rib row K2, [p2, k2] to end.

Rep the last 2 rows 11 times more, and then the first row again.
Cast off in rib.

BUTTONHOLE BAND

With right side facing, beg at neck shaping, using 4.50mm
(US 7) needles and yarn used double, pick up and
k58(66:70:78) sts evenly down left front edge.
1st rib row P2, [k2, p2] to end.
2nd rib row K2, [p2, k2] to end.
3rd row As 1st row.
Buttonhole row K2, p2, k2 tog, yrn, [rib 10, k2 tog, yrn] twice,
rib to end.
Rib 17 rows.
Buttonhole row K2, p2, k2 tog, yrn, [rib 10, k2 tog, yrn] twice,
rib to end.
Rib 3 rows.
Cast off in rib.

COLLAR

Join shoulder seams.
With right side facing, starting at beg of neck shaping, using
4.50mm (US 7) needles and yarn used double, pick up
and k14(15:17:18) sts up right side of front neck, cast on
38(40:40:42) sts, pick up and k14(15:17:18) sts down left side
of front neck. 66(70:74:78) sts.
1st row K4, [p2, k2] to last 6 sts, p2, k4.
2nd row K2, [p2, k2] to end.
Rep the last 2 rows 5(6:7:8) times more.
Change to 5mm (US 8) needles.
Work a further 16(18:20:22) rows.
K 4 rows. Cast off.

TO MAKE UP

Sew cast on edge of collar to cast off sts on back neck. Join
side and sleeve seams. Sew in sleeves. Sew on buttons.

JESPER JUMPER

SKILL LEVEL **Improving / Experienced**

SIZES / MEASUREMENTS

To fit age	3-6	6-12	12-24	24-36	36-48	48-60	mths

ACTUAL GARMENT MEASUREMENTS

Chest	52	56	61	66	72	77	cm
	20 ½	22	24	26	28 ½	30 ½	in
Length to	25	27	30	33	37	41	cm
shoulder	10	10 ½	11 ¾	13	14 ½	16 ¼	in
Sleeve	15	17	19	22	25	28	cm
length	6	6 ¾	7 ½	8 ½	10	11	in

MATERIALS

2(2:2:3:3:3) 50g/1 ¾oz balls in each of MillaMia Naturally Soft Merino in Grass (141) (M) and Snow (124) (B).
2 balls of Midnight (101) (A).
Pair each of 3mm (US 2) and 3.25mm (US 3) knitting needles.

TENSION / GAUGE

25 sts and 34 rows to 10cm/4in square over st st using 3.25mm (US 3) needles.

HINTS AND TIPS

As per the note below when working the diamonds in different colours it is easiest if you wind off a small amount of the colour needed for each diamond from the main balls and leave this hanging behind the piece as you work back and forth, rather than trying to carry any yarn from diamond to diamond.

ABBREVIATIONS

s2kpo – slip two sts, knit one, then pass slipped stitches over – 2 sts decreased
See also page 9.

SUGGESTED ALTERNATIVE COLOURWAYS

Scarlet 140   Forget me not 120   Midnight 101   Plum 162   Snow 124   Claret 104   Fuchsia 143   Petal 122   Midnight 101

NOTE

When working from Chart use small amounts of yarn for each area of colour and twist yarns at back of work to avoid a hole. Right side rows are read from right to left. Wrong side rows are read from left to right. On this chart the 12 st patt is repeated and the edge st is worked.

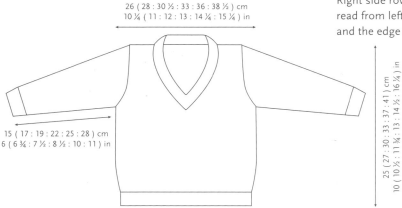

26 (28 : 30 ½ : 33 : 36 : 38 ½) cm
10 ¼ (11 : 12 : 13 : 14 ¼ : 15 ¼) in

15 (17 : 19 : 22 : 25 : 28) cm
6 (6 ¾ : 7 ½ : 8 ½ : 10 : 11) in

25 (27 : 30 : 33 : 37 : 41) cm
10 (10 ½ : 11 ¾ : 13 : 14 ½ : 16 ¼) in

BACK

With 3mm (US 2) needles and A, cast on 66(70:78:82:90:94) sts.
1st rib row K2, [p2, k2] to end.
2nd rib row P2, [k2, p2] to end.
Rep the last 2 rows 3(3:4:4:5:5) times more, inc 1(3:1:3:3:5) sts evenly across last row. 67(73:79:85:93:99) sts.
Change to 3.25mm (US 3) needles.
Break off A.
Join on B.
Beg with a k row, cont in st st until back measures 15(16:18:20:23:26)cm/6(6 ¼:7:8:9:10 ¼)in from cast on edge, ending with a p row.
Shape armholes
Cast off 3(3:4:4:5:5) sts at beg of next 2 rows. 61(67:71:77:83:89) sts.
Next row K2, skpo, k to last 4 sts, k2 tog, k2.
Next row P to end.
Rep the last 2 rows 2(3:3:4:4:5) times. 55(59:63:67:73:77) sts.
Cont in st st until back measures 25(27:30:33:37:41)cm/10(10 ½: 11 ¾:13:14 ½:16 ¼)in from cast on edge, ending with a p row.
Shape shoulders
Cast off 13(14:15:16:18:19) sts at beg of next 2 rows.
Leave rem 29(31:33:35:37:39) sts on a holder.

FRONT

With 3mm (US 2) needles and A, cast on 66(70:78:82:90:94) sts.
1st rib row K2, [p2, k2] to end.
2nd rib row P2, [k2, p2] to end.
Rep the last 2 rows 3(3:4:4:5:5) times more, inc 1(3:1:3:3:5) sts evenly across last row. 67(73:79:85:93:99) sts.
Change to 3.25mm (US 3) needles.
1st row K9(12:9:12:10:1) B, work across 1st row of 12 st patt rep 4(4:5:5:6:8) times, work edge st, k9(12:9:12:10:1) B.
2nd row P9(12:9:12:10:1) B, work across 2nd row edge st, work across 12 st patt rep 4(4:5:5:6:8) times, p9(12:9:12:10:1) B.
These 2 rows set the patt.
Cont in patt until front measures 15(16:18:20:23:26)cm/6(6 ¼: 7:8:9:10 ¼)in from cast on edge, ending with a p row.
Shape armholes
Cast off 3(3:4:4:5:5) sts at beg of next 2 rows.
61(67:71:77:83:89) sts.
Shape front neck
Next row K2, skpo, k22(25:27:30:33:36), k2 tog, k2, turn and work on these sts for first side of front neck.
Next row P to end.
Next row K2, skpo to last 4 sts, k2 tog, k2.
Rep the last 2 rows 1(2:2:3:3:4) times. 24(25:27:28:31:32) sts.
Keeping armhole edge straight cont to dec at neck edge on every alt row until 13(14:15:16:18:19) sts rem.
Cont straight until front measures same as back to shoulder, ending at armhole edge.
Shape shoulder
Cast off.
With right side facing, slip centre st onto a safety pin, join on yarn to rem sts.
Next row K2, skpo, k to last 4 sts, k2 tog, k2.
Next row P to end.
Next row K2, skpo to last 4 sts, k2 tog, k2.
Rep the last 2 rows 1(2:2:3:3:4) times. 24(25:27:28:31:32) sts.

CHART

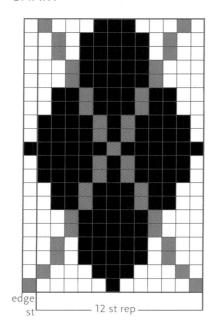

Key
- ▦ M-Grass (141)
- ◼ A-Midnight (101)
- ☐ B-Snow (124)

edge
st ├── 12 st rep ──┤

Keeping armhole edge straight cont to dec at neck edge on every alt row until 13(14:15:16:18:19) sts rem.

Cont straight until front measures same as back to shoulder, ending at armhole edge.

Shape shoulder

Cast off.

SLEEVES

With 3mm (US 2) needles and A cast on 38(38:42:42:46:46) sts.

1st rib row K2, * p2, k2; rep from * to end.

2nd rib row P2, * k2, p2; rep from * to end.

Rep the last 2 rows 3(3:4:4:5:5) times more, inc 2 sts evenly across last row on **2nd, 4th and 6th sizes** only. 38(40:42:44:46:48) sts.

Change to 3.25mm (US 3) needles.

Break off A.

Join on M.

Beg with a k row, cont in st st.

Work 4(4:6:6:8:8) rows.

Inc row K3, m1, k to last 3 sts, m1, k3.

Work 3 rows.

Rep the last 4 rows 7(8:10:11:13:14) times more, and then the inc row again.

56(60:66:70:76:80) sts.

Cont straight until sleeve measures 15(17:19:22:25:28)cm/ 6(6 ¾:7 ½: 8 ½:10:11)in from cast on edge, ending with a p row.

Shape sleeve top

Cast off 3(3:4:4:5:5) sts at beg of next 2 rows.

50(54:58:62:66:70) sts.

Next row K2, skpo, k to last 4 sts, k2 tog, k2.

Next row P to end.

Rep the last 2 rows 2(3:3:4:4:5) times. 44(46:50:52:56:58) sts.

Cast off 4 sts at beg of next 8(8:10:10:10:12) rows.

Cast off.

NECKBAND

Join right shoulder seam.

With right side facing, using 3mm (US 3) needles and A, pick up and k32(36:38:42:44:48) sts evenly down left side of front neck, k one st from safety pin, pick up and k32(34:38:40:44:46) sts evenly up right side of front neck, k sts from back neck holder dec one st in centre. 93(101:109:117:125:133) sts.

1st, 2nd, 5th and 6th sizes only

1st row [P2, k2] 15(16:-:-:20:21) times, p1, [k2, p2] to end.

3rd and 4th sizes only

1st row [K2, p2] –(-:17:18:-:-) times, k2, p1, k2, [p2, k2] to end.

All sizes

This row sets the rib.

2nd row Rib 31(35:37:41:43:47), s2kpo, rib to end.

3rd row Rib to end.

4th row Rib 30(34:36:40:42:46), s2kpo, rib to end.

5th row Rib to end.

6th row Rib 29(33:35:39:41:45), s2kpo, rib to end.

7th row Rib to end.

3rd, 4th, 5th and 6th sizes only

8th row Rib -(-:34:38:40:44), s2kpo, rib to end.

9th row Rib to end.

5th and 6th sizes only

10th row Rib -(-:-:-:39:43), s2kpo, rib to end.

11th row Rib to end.

All sizes

Cast off in rib, dec on this row as before.

TO MAKE UP

Join right shoulder seam and neckband. Join side and sleeve seams. Sew in sleeves.

JESSI SCARF

SKILL LEVEL **Beginner**

SIZES /MEASUREMENTS

To fit age   One size

ACTUAL MEASUREMENTS

Length	102	cm
	40	in
Width	12	cm
	4 ¾	in

MATERIALS

Two 50g/1 ¾oz balls of MillaMia Naturally Soft Merino in Lilac Blossom (123).
Pair of 3.25mm (US 3) needles.

TENSION / GAUGE

25 sts and 50 rows to 10cm/4in over g-st using 3.25mm (US 3) needles.

HINTS AND TIPS

A simple beginners knit this scarf is a good way to get used to the different textures that are possible to create in knitted fabric. The moss stitch border frames the garter stitch body beautifully, and ensures a reversible fabric that lies flat and does not curl as stocking stitch sometimes can.

ABBREVIATIONS

See page 9.

SUGGESTED ALTERNATIVE COLOURWAYS

| Scarlet 140 | Forget me not 120 | Petal 122 | Peacock 144 | Snow 124 |

SCARF

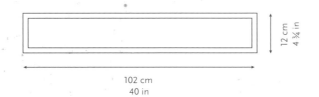

102 cm
40 in

12 cm
4 ¾ in

With 3.25mm (US 3) needles cast on 31 sts.
Moss st row K1, [p1, k1] to end.
Rep the last row 9 times more.
Patt row [K1, p1] 3 times, k to last 6 sts, [p1, k1] 3 times.
Rep the last row until scarf measures 100cm/39 ½in from cast on edge.
Moss st row K1, [p1, k1] to end.
Rep the last row 9 times more.
Cast off in moss st.

From left to right: **Mattias Cardigan**
in Scarlet (140), Forget me not (120), Seaside (161)
and Midnight (101) pattern on page 68 and
Max Babygrow in Scarlet (140), Forget me not (120)
and Midnight (101) pattern on page 62

MAX
BABYGROW
MATTIAS
CARDIGAN

MAX BABYGROW

SKILL LEVEL **Improving / Experienced**

SIZES / MEASUREMENTS

To fit age	0-3	3-6	6-12	months

ACTUAL GARMENT MEASUREMENTS

Chest	53	56	60	cm
	21	22	23 ½	in
Length to shoulder	44	48	53	cm
	17 ¼	19	21	in
Sleeve length	14	16	18	cm
	5 ½	6 ¼	7	in
Inside leg length	12	14	17	cm
	4 ¾	5 ½	6 ¾	in

MATERIALS

3(4:5) 50g/1 ¾oz balls of MillaMia Naturally Soft Merino in Forget me not (120) (M).
1(2:2) balls of Scarlet (140) (A).
One ball of Midnight (101) (B).
Pair each of 2.75mm (US 2) and 3.25mm (US 3) knitting needles.
13 buttons approx 15mm/½in in diameter.

TENSION / GAUGE

25 sts and 34 rows to 10cm/4in square over st st using 3.25mm (US 3) needles.

HINTS AND TIPS

We have shown the Max in quite gender specific colours in these photos. Try it also in the other suggested colourway if you want a more unisex result. Remember to block the pocket nice and flat before you sew it on and we find mattress stitch gives the neatest result when finishing this item. The Max is quite a wide, loose fit – plenty of room for well-fed babies!

ABBREVIATIONS

See page 9.

SUGGESTED ALTERNATIVE COLOURWAYS

Petal 122   Fuchsia 143   Peacock 144   Snow 124   Putty Grey 121   Daisy Yellow 142

26 ½ (28 : 30) cm
10 ½ (11 : 11 ¾) in

14 (16 : 18) cm
5 ½ (6 ¼ : 7) in

44 (48 : 53) cm
17 ¼ (19 : 21) in

12 (14 : 17) cm
4 ¾ (5 ½ : 6 ¾) in

BACK

First leg

With 2.75mm (US 2) needles and B, cast on 22(24:26) sts.

Rib row [K1, p1] to end.

Rep the last row for 2(3:4)cm/¾(1 ¼:1 ½)in, ending with a right side row.

Inc row Rib 3(2:1), [m1, rib 4] 4(5:6) times, m1, rib 3(2:1). 27(30:33) sts.

Cut off B.

Join on M.

Change to 3.25mm (US 3) needles.

Beg with a k row cont in st st.

Work 2(2:4) rows.

Inc row K4, m1, k to end.

P 1 row.

Rep the last 2 rows 14 times more, and then the inc row again. 43(46:49) sts.

Cont straight until leg measures 12(14:17)cm/4 ¾(5 ½:6 ¾)in ending with a p row.

Shape crotch

Next row Cast off 4 sts, k to end. 39(42:45) sts.

P 1 row.

Leave these sts on a holder.

Second leg

With 2.75mm (US 2) needles and B, cast on 22(24:26) sts.

Rib row [K1, p1] to end.

Rep the last row for 2(3:4)cm/¾(1 ¼:1 ½)in, ending with a right side row.

Inc row Rib 3(2:1), [m1, rib 4] 4(5:6) times, m1, rib 3(2:1). 27(30:33) sts.

Cut off B.

Join on M.

Change to 3.25mm (US 3) needles.

Beg with a k row cont in st st.

Work 2(2:4) rows.

Inc row K to last 4 sts, m1, k4.

P 1 row.

Rep the last 2 rows 14 times more, and then the inc row again. 43(46:49) sts.

Cont straight until leg measures 12(14:17)cm/4 ¾(5 ½:6 ¾)in ending with a k row.

Shape crotch

Next row Cast off 4 sts, p to end. 39(42:45) sts.

Next row K38(41:44), k last st tog with first st on first leg, k38(41:44). 77(83:89) sts.

Next row P to end.

Next row K34(36:38), skpo, k5(7:9), k2 tog, k34(36:38).

Next row P to end.

Next row K34(36:38), skpo, k3(5:7), k2 tog, k34(36:38).

Next row P to end.

Next row K34(36:38), skpo, k1(3:5), k2 tog, k34(36:38).

2nd and 3rd sizes only

Next row P to end.

Next row K-(36:38), skpo, k-(1:3), k2 tog, k-(36:38).

3rd size only

Next row P to end.

Next row K-(-:38), skpo, k-(-:1), k2 tog, k-(-:38).

All sizes

Next row P to end.

Next row K34(36:38), s1 1, k2 tog, psso, k34(36:38). 69(73:77) sts.

Cont straight until back measures 32(35:38)cm/12 ½(13 ¾:15)in from cast on edges, ending with a p row **.

Shape armholes

Cast off 4 sts at beg of next 2 rows. 61(65:69) sts.

Dec row K4, skpo, k to last 6 sts, k2 tog, k4.

Next row P to end.

Rep the last 2 rows until 27(29:31) sts rem, ending with a dec row.

Cut off M.

Join on B.

Next row P to end.

Change to 2.75mm (US 2) needles.

1st rib row P1, [k1, p1] to end.

2nd rib row K1, [p1, k1] to end.

Rep the last 2 rows 2(3:4) times more.

Cast off in rib.

FRONT

Work as given for back to **.
Shape armholes
Cast off 6 sts at beg of next 2 rows. 57(61:65) sts.
Next row K2, skpo, k to last 4 sts, k2 tog, k2.
Next row P to end.
Rep the last 2 rows until 23(25:27) sts rem, ending with a dec row.
Cut off M.
Join on B.
Next row P to end.
Change to 2.75mm (US 2) needles.
1st rib row P1, [k1, p1] to end.
2nd rib row K1, [p1, k1] to end.
Rep the last 2 rows 2(3:4) times more.
Cast off in rib.

RIGHT SLEEVE

With 2.75mm (US 2) needles and B cast on 34(36:38) sts.
Rib row [K1, p1] to end.
Rep the last row for 2(3:4)cm/¾(1 ¼:1 ½)in, ending with a wrong side row, inc one st at centre of last row. 35(37:39) sts.
Cut off B.
Join on A.
Change to 3.25mm (US 3) needles.
Beg with a k row cont in st st.
Work 2(2:6) rows.
Inc row K3, m1, k to last 3 sts, m1, k3.
Work 5(5:3) rows.
Rep the last 6(6:4) rows 4(5:7) times more, and then the inc row again. 47(51:57) sts.
Cont straight until sleeve measures 14(16:18)cm/5 ½(6 ¼:7)in from cast on edge, ending with a p row ***.
Shape sleeve top
Next row Cast off 6 sts, k to end.
Next row Cast off 4 sts, p to end. 37(41:47) sts.
Next row K2, skpo, k to last 6 sts, k2 tog, k4.

Next row P to end.
Next row K to end.
Next row P to end.
Rep the last 4 rows 3(3:2) times more. 29(33:41) sts.
Next row K2, skpo, k to last 6 sts, k2 tog, k4.
Next row P to end.
Rep the last 2 rows until 11(13:15) sts rem, ending with a dec row.
Cut off M.
Join on B.
Next row P to end.
Change to 2.75mm (US 2) needles.
1st rib row P1, [k1, p1] to end.
2nd rib row K1, [p1, k1] to end.
Rep the last 2 rows 2(3:4) times more.
Cast off in rib.

LEFT SLEEVE

Work as given for right sleeve to ***.
Shape sleeve top
Next row Cast off 4 sts, k to end.
Next row Cast off 6 sts, p to end. 37(41:47) sts.
Next row K4, skpo, k to last 4 sts, k2 tog, k2.
Next row P to end.
Next row K to end.
Next row P to end.
Rep the last 4 rows 3(3:2) times more. 29(33:41) sts.
Dec row K4, skpo, k to last 4 sts, k2 tog, k2.
Next row P to end.
Rep the last 2 rows until 11(13:15) sts rem, ending with a dec row.
Cut off M.
Join on B.
Next row P to end.
Change to 2.75mm (US 2) needles.
1st rib row P1, [k1, p1] to end.
2nd rib row K1, [p1, k1] to end.
Rep the last 2 rows 2(3:4) times more.
Cast off in rib.

POCKET

With 3.25mm (US 3) needles and A, cast on 39(43:47) sts.
Beg with a k row work 18(20:22) rows in st st.
Shape top
Next row K2, skpo, k to last 4 sts, k2 tog, k2.
Next row P to end.
Rep the last 2 rows until 19(21:23) sts rem.
Cast off.
Edgings (both alike)
With right side facing, using 2.75mm (US 2) needles and B
pick up and k21(23:25) sts evenly along shaped edge.
1st rib row P1, [k1, p1] to end.
2nd rib row K1, [p1, k1] to end.
Rep the last 2 rows once more, and then the first row again.
Cast off in rib.

SLEEVE BUTTON BAND (one on each sleeve)

With right side facing, using 2.75mm (US 2) needles and B
pick up and k31(33:35) sts evenly along front sleeve edge –
between cast off for sleeve shaping and cast off at top.
1st rib row P1, [k1, p1] to end.
2nd rib row K1, [p1, k1] to end.
Rep the last 2 rows once more, and then the first row again.
Cast off in rib.

FRONT BUTTONHOLE BAND
(work twice – along both front raglan edges)

With right side facing, using 2.75mm (US 2) needles and B
pick up and k31(33:35) sts evenly along front raglan edge.
1st rib row P1, [k1, p1] to end.
2nd rib row K1, [p1, k1] to end.
Left front band
Buttonhole row Rib 3, yrn, rib 2 tog, [rib 8(9:10), yrn, rib2 tog]
twice, rib 6.

Right front band
Buttonhole row Rib 7, yrn, rib 2 tog, [rib 8(9:10), yrn, rib2 tog]
twice, rib 2.
Both bands
Rib 2 more rows.
Cast off in rib.

LEG BUTTON BAND

Join cast off edges to form crotch seam.
With right side facing, using 2.75mm (US 2) needles and B
pick up and k71(83:95) sts evenly along back leg edges.
1st rib row P1, [k1, p1] to end.
2nd rib row K1, [p1, k1] to end.
Rep the last 2 rows once more, and then the first row again.
Cast off in rib.

LEG BUTTONHOLE BAND

With right side facing, using 2.75mm (US 2) needles and B
pick up and k71(83:95) sts evenly along front leg edges.
1st rib row P1, [k1, p1] to end.
2nd rib row K1, [p1, k1] to end.
Buttonhole row Rib 5, yrn, rib2 tog, [rib 8(10:12), yrn, rib2 tog]
3 times, rib 7(9:11), rib2 tog, yrn, [rib 8(10:12), rib2 tog, yrn]
twice, rib 5.
Rib 2 more rows.
Cast off in rib.

MAKE UP

Join side and sleeve seams. Join back raglan seams. Join under
arm seam. Lap buttonhole bands over button bands and sew
in place. Sew on buttons.

MATTIAS CARDIGAN

SKILL LEVEL Beginner / Improving

SIZES / MEASUREMENTS

To fit age	1-2	2-3	3-4	4-5	years

ACTUAL GARMENT MEASUREMENTS

Chest	58	62	68	72	cm
	23	24 ½	26 ¾	28 ½	in
Length to	28	32	36	40	cm
back neck	11	12 ½	14 ¼	15 ¾	in
Sleeve	21	24	26	28	cm
length	8 ¼	9 ½	10 ¼	11	in

MATERIALS

1(1:2:2) 50g/1 ¾oz balls of MillaMia Naturally Soft Merino in Midnight (101) (A).
2(2:2:3) balls of Scarlet (140) (B).
2 balls of Forget me not (120) (C).
1(1:1:2) balls of Seaside (161) (D).
Pair each of 3mm (US 2) and 3.25mm (US 3) knitting needles.
Circular 3mm (US 2) knitting needle.
2 buttons approx 15mm/½in in diameter.
4 buttons approx 20mm/¾in in diameter.

TENSION / GAUGE

25 sts and 34 rows to 10cm/4in square over st st using 3.25mm (US 3) needles.

ABBREVIATIONS

See page 9.

HINTS AND TIPS

This is a playful and fun knit, and good for a developing knitter who has mastered basic cardigans and now wants to get more adventurous with their next project. There are buttons both on the button stand on the front and also two smaller buttons as a design feature on the pockets.

SUGGESTED ALTERNATIVE COLOURWAYS

Storm	Scarlet	Snow	Seaside		Midnight	Claret	Fawn	Forget me not
102	140	124	161		101	103	160	120

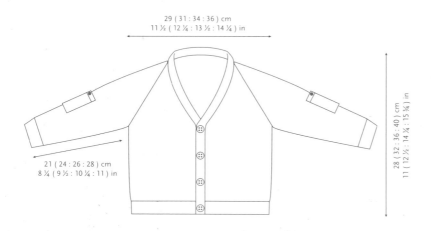

29 (31 : 34 : 36) cm
11 ½ (12 ¼ : 13 ½ : 14 ¼) in

21 (24 : 26 : 28) cm
8 ¼ (9 ½ : 10 ¼ : 11) in

28 (32 : 36 : 40) cm
11 (12 ½ : 14 ¼ : 15 ¾) in

BACK

With 3mm (US 2) needles and A cast on 74(80:86:92) sts.
1st rib row K2, [p1, k2] to end.
2nd rib row P2, [k1, p2] to end.
Rep the last 2 rows 7 times more.
Cut off A.
Join on B.
Change to 3.25mm (US 3) needles.
Beg with a k row, cont in st st until back measures
16(19:22:25)cm/6 ¼(7 ½:8 ¾:9 ¾)in from cast on edge,
ending with a p row.
Shape raglan armholes
Cast off 4 sts at beg of next 2 rows. 66(72:78:84) sts.
Next row K1, skpo, k to last 3 sts, k2 tog, k1.
Next row P to end.
Rep the last 2 rows until 28(30:32:34) sts rem, ending with a p row.
Cast off.

LEFT FRONT

With 3mm (US 2) needles and A cast on 33(36:39:42) sts.
1st rib row [K2, p1] to end.
2nd rib row [K1, p2] to end.
Rep the last 2 rows 7 times more.
Cut off A.
Join on C.
Change to 3.25mm (US 3) needles.
Beg with a k row, cont in st st until front measures
16(19:22:25)cm/6 ¼(7 ½:8 ¾:9 ¾)in from cast on edge,
ending with a p row.
Shape raglan armhole and front neck
Next row Cast off 4 sts, k to last 3 sts, k2 tog, k1.
Next row P to end.
Next row K1, skpo, k to end.
Next row P to end.
Next row K1, skpo, k to last 3 sts, k2 tog, k1.
Next row P to end.

Rep the last 4 rows 6(7:8:9) times more.
Keeping neck edge straight cont to dec at armhole edge until
2 sts rem, ending with a p row.
Cast off.

RIGHT FRONT

With 3mm (US 2) needles and A cast on 33(36:39:42) sts.
1st rib row [P1, k2] to end.
2nd rib row [P2, k1] to end.
Rep the last 2 rows 7 times more.
Cut off A.
Change to 3.25mm (US 3) needles.
Beg with a k row, cont in st st and stripes of 4 rows D and
4 rows B until front measures 16(19:22:25)cm/6 ¼(7 ½:8 ¾:9 ¾)in
from cast on edge, ending with a p row.
Shape raglan armhole and front neck
Next row K1, skpo, k to end.
Next row Cast off 4 sts, p to end.
Next row K to last 3 sts, k2 tog, k1.
Next row P to end.
Next row K1, skpo, k to last 3 sts, k2 tog, k1.
Next row P to end.
Rep the last 4 rows 6(7:8:9) times more.
Keeping neck edge straight cont to dec at armhole edge until
2 sts rem, ending with a p row.
Cast off.

LEFT SLEEVE

With 3mm (US 2) needles and A cast on 41(44:47:50) sts.
1st rib row K2, [p1, k2] to end.
2nd rib row P2, [k1, p2] to end.
Rep the last 2 rows 7 times more.
Cut off A.

Change to 3.25mm (US 3) needles.

Beg with a k row, cont in st st and stripes of 4 rows D and 4 rows B **at the same time** work increases as folls:

Work 2 rows.

Inc row K3, m1, k to last 3 sts, m1, k3.

Work 5 rows.

Rep the last 6 rows 6(7:8:9) times more, and then the inc row again. 57(62:67:72) sts.

Cont straight until sleeve measures 21(24:26:28)cm/8 ¼ (9 ½: 10 ¼:11)in from cast on edge, ending with a p row.

Shape sleeve top

Cast off 4 sts at beg of next 2 rows. 49(54:59:64) sts.

Next row K2, skpo, k to last 4 sts, k2 tog, k2.

Next row P to end.

Rep the last 2 rows until 11(12:13:14) sts rem, ending with a p row.

Cast off.

RIGHT SLEEVE

With 3mm (US 2) needles and A cast on 41(44:47:50) sts.

1st rib row K2, [p1, k2] to end.

2nd rib row P2, [k1, p2] to end.

Rep the last 2 rows 7 times more.

Cut off A.

Join on C.

Using C only complete as for left sleeve.

LEFT POCKET

With 3.25mm (US 3) needles and C cast on 19(19:22:22) sts.

Beg with a k row work 28(28:30:30) rows in st st.

Cut off C.

Join on A.

1st rib row P1, [k2, p1] to end.

2nd rib row K1, [p2, k1] to end.

Rep the last 2 rows twice more.

Cast off in rib.

RIGHT POCKET

Work as given for left pocket using B instead of C.

FRONT BAND

Join raglan seams.

With right side facing, 3mm (US 2) circular needle and A, pick up and k40(48:56:64) sts up right front edge, to beg of neck shaping, 30(33:36:39) sts along right front neck edge, 9(10:11:12) sts across top of right sleeve, 27(30:30:33)sts from back neck, 9(10:11:12) sts across top of left sleeve, 30(33:36:39) sts down left front neck edge to beg of neck shaping, 40(48:56:64) sts along left front edge. 185(212:236:263) sts.

1st rib row P2, [k1, p2] to end.

2nd rib row K2, [p1, k2] to end.

Rib 2 more rows.

Buttonhole row Rib 3, [work2 tog, y2rn, work2 tog, rib 7(9:11:13)] 3 times, work2 tog, y2rn, work2 tog, rib to end.

Rib 4 more rows.

Cast off in rib.

TO MAKE UP

Sew on pockets. Join side and sleeve seams. Sew on smaller buttons to centre of pocket rib and larger buttons to front band.

OLIVER SLEEPING BAG

SKILL LEVEL Beginner

SIZES / MEASUREMENTS

| To fit age | 0-6 | months |

ACTUAL MEASUREMENTS

| Chest | 61 | cm |
| | 24 | in |

| Length to | 72 | cm |
| shoulder | 28 ½ | in |

MATERIALS

Three 50g/1 ¾oz balls of MillaMia Naturally Soft Merino in Scarlet (140) (A).
Four balls of Peacock (144) (B).
Pair each of 3mm (US 2) and 3.25mm (US 3) knitting needles.
2 buttons approx 21mm/⅞ in in diameter.

TENSION / GAUGE

25 sts and 34 rows to 10cm/4in square over st st using 3.25mm (US 3) needles.

HINTS AND TIPS

Who wouldn't want a homemade sleeping bag made from extra fine merino wool? Such a nice gift for anyone expecting a new baby – have lots of fun choosing suitable colours.

ABBREVIATIONS

See page 9.

SUGGESTED ALTERNATIVE COLOURWAYS

| Plum | Snow | | Claret | Plum | | Seaside | Fawn |
| 162 | 124 | | 104 | 162 | | 161 | 160 |

30 ½ cm
12 in

72 cm
28 ½ in

BACK

With 3.25mm (US 3) needles and A, cast on 116 sts.
Beg with a k row, cont in st st and stripes of 22 rows A and
22 rows B **at the same time** shape sides as follows:
Work 6 rows.
Dec row K10, skpo, k to last 12 sts, k2 tog, k10.
Work 9 rows.
Rep the last 10 rows 17 times more, and then the dec row
again. 78 sts.
Work 7 rows.
Shape armholes
Cast off 6 sts at beg of next 2 rows. 66 sts **.
Next row K2, skpo, k to last 4 sts, k2 tog, k2.
Next row P to end.
Rep the last 2 rows 3 times more. 58 sts.
Work a further 30 rows.
Shape back neck
Next row K15, turn and work on these sts.
*** Dec one st at neck edge on next 5 rows. 10 sts.
Work 2 rows, ending with 22 rows A.
This is the shoulder line.
Cont in A, work 2 rows.
1st buttonhole row K4, cast off 2 sts, k4.
2nd buttonhole row P4, cast on 2 sts, p4.
Work 2 rows.
Cut off A.
Join on B.
Change to 3mm (US 2) needles.
1st row K3, m1, k4, m1, k3. 12 sts.
2nd row P3, k2, p2, k2, p3.
3rd row K3, p2, k2, p2, k3.
Work a further 2 rows.
Cast off in rib ***.
With right side facing slip centre 28 sts on a holder, rejoin yarn
to rem sts, k to end.
Work from *** to ***.

FRONT

Work as given for back to **. 66 sts.
Shape front neck
Next row K2, skpo, k24, k2 tog, k2, turn and work on these sts
for first side of front neck.
Next row P to end.
Next row K2, skpo to last 4 sts, k2 tog, k2.
Rep the last 2 rows twice more. 24 sts.
Keeping armhole edge straight cont to dec at neck edge on
every right side row until 10 sts rem.
Work 11 rows straight ending with 22 rows A.
Cast off.
With right side facing, slip centre 2 sts onto a safety pin, join
on yarn to rem sts.
Next row K2, skpo, k to last 4 sts, k2 tog, k2.
Next row P to end.
Next row K2, skpo to last 4 sts, k2 tog, k2.
Rep the last 2 rows twice more. 24 sts.
Keeping armhole edge straight cont to dec at neck edge on
every right side row until 10 sts rem.
Work 11 rows straight ending with 22 rows A.
Cast off.

FRONT NECKBAND

With right side facing, using 3mm (US 2) needles and B, pick up and k36 sts evenly down left side of front neck, k2 from safety pin, pick up and k36 sts evenly up right side of front neck. 74 sts.

1st row P2, [k2, p2] to end.
This row sets the rib.
2nd row Rib 35, k2 tog, skpo, rib to end.
3rd row Rib 34, p2 tog tbl, p2 tog, rib to end.
4th row Rib 33, k2 tog, skpo, rib to end.
Cast off in rib, dec on this row as before.

BACK NECKBAND

With right side facing, using 3mm (US 2) needles and B, pick up and k17 sts down right side of back neck, k28 sts from back neck holder, pick up and k17 sts up left side of back neck. 62 sts.

1st row P2, [k2, p2] to end.
2nd row K2, [p2, k2] to end.
Rep these 2 rows once more.
Cast off in rib.

LEFT ARMBAND

Join side and bottom seams.
With right side facing, using 3mm (US 2) needles and B, pick up and k51 sts evenly down back armhole edge and 43 sts up front armhole edge. 94 sts.

1st row K2, [p2, k2] to end.
This row sets the rib.
Work a further 3 rows.
Cast off in rib.

RIGHT ARMBAND

With right side facing, using 3mm (US 2) needles and B, pick up and k43 sts evenly down front armhole edge and 51 sts up back armhole edge. 94 sts.

1st row K2, [p2, k2] to end.
This row sets the rib.
Work a further 3 rows.
Cast off in rib.

TO MAKE UP

Sew on buttons.

LARS JUMPER

SKILL LEVEL **Improving**

SIZES / MEASUREMENTS

| To fit age | 1-2 | 2-3 | 3-4 | 4-5 | years |

ACTUAL GARMENT MEASUREMENTS

Chest	58	64	68	72	cm
	23	25	26 ¾	28 ¼	in
Length to	28	31	34	37	cm
shoulder	11	12 ¼	13 ½	14 ½	in
Sleeve	21	24	26	28	cm
length	8 ¼	9 ½	10 ¼	11	in

MATERIALS

2(3:4:5) 50g/1 ¾oz balls of MillaMia Naturally Soft Merino in Forget me not (120) (M).
1(2:2:3) balls of Seaside (161) (A).
One ball in each of Daisy Yellow (142) (B) and Snow (124) (C).
Pair each of 3mm (US 2) and 3.25mm (US 3) knitting needles.
Circular 3mm (US 2) knitting needle.
3 buttons approx 15mm/½in in diameter.

TENSION / GAUGE

25 sts and 34 rows to 10cm/4in square over st st using 3.25mm (US 3) needles.

HINTS AND TIPS

This is a great basic shape for a jumper. If you are not a Fair Isle enthusiast you can always replace the colourwork section with a simple stripe. Press the collar nice and flat before you sew it to the back.

ABBREVIATIONS

See page 9.

SUGGESTED ALTERNATIVE COLOURWAYS

| Fawn 160 | Storm 102 | Claret 104 | Snow 124 | | Petal 122 | Fuchsia 143 | Forget me not 120 | Snow 124 |

NOTE

When working from Chart all rows are read from right to left, after working the centre st (last st on left hand side) read the chart from left to right, omitting the centre st.

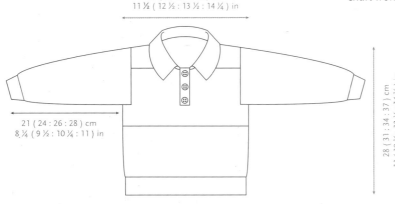

29 (32 : 34 : 36) cm
11 ½ (12 ½ : 13 ½ : 14 ¼) in

21 (24 : 26 : 28) cm
8 ¼ (9 ½ : 10 ¼ : 11) in

28 (31: 34 : 37) cm
11 (12 ¼ : 13 ½ : 14 ½) in

BACK

With 3mm (US 2) needles and A cast on 74(80:86:92) sts.
1st rib row K2, [p1, k2] to end.
2nd rib row P2, [k1, p2] to end.
Rep the last 2 rows 7(8:9:10) times more, inc one st at centre of last row. 75(81:87:93) sts.
Cut off A. Join on M. Change to 3.25mm (US 3) needles.
Beg with a k row work in st st. Work 22(32:44:50) rows.
Now beg working from Chart. Work 20(16:10:10) rows.
Shape armholes
Cast off 6(7:8:9) sts at beg of next 2 rows. 63(67:71:75) sts. **
Cont in patt to end of Chart.
Cont in M until armhole measures 12(13:14:15)cm/4 ¾(5:5 ½:6)in, ending with a p row.
Shape shoulders
Cast off 8(8:9:9) sts at beg of next 2 rows and 8(9:9:10) sts at beg of foll 2 rows. Leave rem 31(33:35:37) sts on a holder.

FRONT

Work as given for back to **.
Divide for front opening
Next row Patt 29(31:33:35), turn and work on these sts for first side of front neck.
Cont in patt to end of Chart.
Cont in M. Work 2 rows, ending with a k row.
Shape neck
Next row Cast off 6(7:8:9) sts, patt to end. 23(24:25:26) sts.
Dec one st at neck edge on the next 7 rows. 16(17:18:19) sts.
Cont straight until front measures same as back to shoulder ending at armhole edge.
Shape shoulder
Cast off 8(8:9:9) sts at beg of next row.
Work 1 row. Cast off rem 8(9:9:10) sts.
With right side facing, join on yarn, cast off centre 5 sts, patt to end.
Cont in patt to end of Chart.
Cont in M. Work 3 rows, ending with a p row.
Shape neck
Next row Cast off 6(7:8:9) sts, patt to end. 23(24:25:26) sts.

Dec one st at neck edge on the next 7 rows. 16(17:18:19) sts.
Cont straight until front measures same as back to shoulder ending at armhole edge.
Shape shoulder
Cast off 8(8:9:9) sts at beg of next row.
Work 1 row. Cast off rem 8(9:9:10) sts.

SLEEVES

With 3mm (US 2) needles and A cast on 41(44:47:53) sts.
1st rib row K2, [p1, k2] to end.
2nd rib row P2, [k1, p2] to end.
Rep the last 2 rows 7 times more.
Cut off A. Join on M. Change to 3.25mm (US 3) needles.
Beg with a k row work in st st.
Work 2 rows.
Inc row K3, m1, k to last 3 sts, m1, k3.
Work 5 rows.
Rep the last 6 rows 6(7:8:9) times more, and then the inc row again. 57(62:67:75) sts.
Cont straight until sleeve measures 21(24:26:28)cm/8 ¼ (9 ½:10 ¼:11)in from cast on edge, ending with a p row.
Mark each end of last row with a coloured thread.
Work a further 8(8:10:10) rows. Cast off.

BUTTON BAND

With right side facing, using 3mm (US 2) needles and A, pick up and k25(27:29:31) sts evenly along right front edge.
1st row K1, [p1, k1] to end.
2nd row P1, [k1, p1] to end.
Rep the last 2 rows twice more, and then the first row again.
Cast off in rib.

BUTTONHOLE BAND

With right side facing, using 3mm (US 2) needles and A, pick up and k25(27:29:31) sts evenly along left front edge.
1st row K1, [p1, k1] to end.
2nd row P1, [k1, p1] to end.

CHART

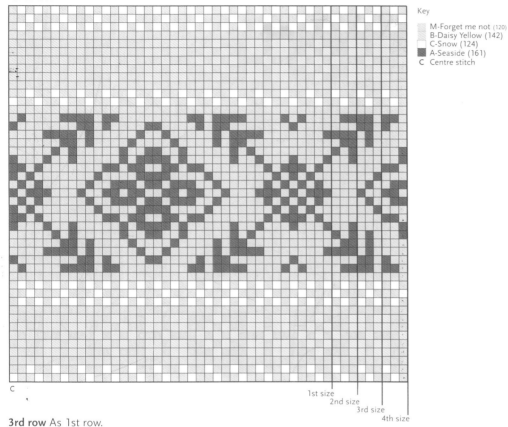

Key
M-Forget me not (120)
B-Daisy Yellow (142)
C-Snow (124)
A-Seaside (161)
C Centre stitch

1st size
2nd size
3rd size
4th size

C

3rd row As 1st row.
Buttonhole row Rib 3, [yrn, rib2 tog, rib 6(7:8:9)] twice, yrn, rib2 tog, rib 4.
Rib 3 rows. Cast off in rib.

COLLAR

With 3mm (US 2) needles and A cast on 33(39:45:51) sts.
Rib row K1, [p1, k1] to end.
Next row Cast on 6 sts, [p1, k1] 3 times across these sts, then rib to end.
Next row Cast on 6sts, [k1,p1] 3 times across these sts, then rib to end.

Rep the last 2 rows 4 times more. 93(99:105:111) sts.
Change to 3.25mm (US 3) needles.
Cont in rib until collar measures 9cm/3 ½in from cast on edge.
Cast off in rib.

TO MAKE UP

Sew on sleeves joining rows after markers to cast off sections underarm. Join side and sleeve seams. Place lower edge of left front band over lower edge of right front band and sew in place. Starting and ending halfway across front bands sew cast on edge of collar to neck edge. Sew on buttons.

From left to right:
Kasper Jacket in Moss (103)
pattern on page 82
and **Kalle Tank Top** in Claret (104)
and Fawn (160) pattern on page 88

KASPER
JACKET
KALLE
TANK TOP

KASPER JACKET

SKILL LEVEL Improving

SIZES / MEASUREMENTS

To fit age	2-3	3-4	4-5	5-6	6-7	years

ACTUAL GARMENT MEASUREMENTS

Chest	58	62	68	72	76	cm
	23	24 ½	27	28 ½	30	in
Length	28	32	36	40	44	cm
to shoulder	11	12 ½	14 ¼	15 ¾	17 ½	in
Sleeve	24	27	30	33	36	cm
length	9 ½	10 ½	11 ¾	13	14 ¼	in

MATERIALS

5 (6:7:8:9) 50g/1 ¾oz balls of MillaMia Naturally Soft Merino in Scarlet (140).
Pair each of 3mm (US 2) and 3.25mm (US 3) knitting needles.
Circular 3mm (US 2) knitting needle.
8 (8:8:10:10) buttons approx 20mm/¾in in diameter.
7 (7:7:9:9) small poppers.

TENSION / GAUGE

25 sts and 34 rows to 10cm/4in square over st st using 3.25mm (US 3) needles.

HINTS AND TIPS

Kasper is the answer to every mother's dream. Cool and contemporary it looks great, but made in our Naturally Soft Merino wool it is also warm and comforting. Stunning and versatile it is a great unisex item. The buttons are just decorative – it is the poppers on the inside that do the fastening and enable you to specify either a boy or girl style opening. Please note it might be helpful when knitting the collar to remember that as always with knitting patterns when 'left' and 'right' are mentioned this refers to the 'left side as worn' or the 'right side as worn'.

ABBREVIATIONS

See page 9.

SUGGESTED ALTERNATIVE COLOURWAYS

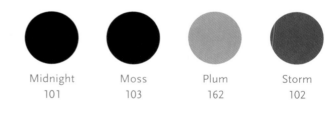

Midnight	Moss	Plum	Storm
101	103	162	102

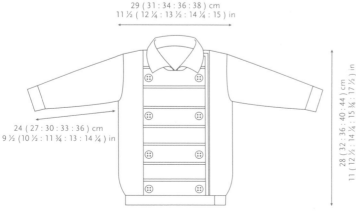

29 (31 : 34 : 36 : 38) cm
11 ½ (12 ¼ : 13 ½ : 14 ¼ : 15) in

24 (27 : 30 : 33 : 36) cm
9 ½ (10 ½ : 11 ¾ : 13 : 14 ¼) in

28 (32 : 36 : 40 : 44) cm
11 (12 ½ : 14 ¼ : 15 ¾ : 17 ½) in

BACK

With 3mm (US 2) needles cast on 74(80:86:92:98) sts.
1st rib row P2, [k4, p2] to end.
2nd rib row K2, [p4, k2] to end.
Rep the last 2 rows 7 times more.
Change to 3.25mm (US 3) needles.
Beg with a k row, cont in st st until back measures
16(19:22:25:28)cm/6 ¼(7 ½:8 ¾:9 ¾:11)in from cast on edge,
ending with a p row.
Shape armholes
Cast off 3(3:4:4:5) sts at beg of next 2 rows. 68(74:78:84:88) sts.
Next row K2, skpo, k to last 4 sts, k2 tog, k2.
Next row P to end.
Rep the last 2 rows 5(6:6:7:7) times. 56(60:64:68:72) sts.
Cont in st st until back measures 28(32:36:40:44)cm/11(12 ½:
14 ¼:15 ¾:17 ½)in from cast on edge, ending with a p row.
Shape shoulders
Cast off 6(7:7:8:8) sts at beg of next 2 rows and 7(7:8:8:9) sts
at beg of foll 2 rows.
Leave rem 30(32:34:36:38) sts on a holder.

LEFT FRONT

With 3mm (US 2) needles cast on 62(68:74:80:86) sts.
1st rib row P2, [k4, p2] to end.
2nd rib row P6, k2, [p4, k2] to end.
Rep the last 2 rows 6 times more, and then the first row again.
Next row Cast off 4(6:8:10:12) sts, rib to end. 58(62:66:70:74) sts.
Change to 3.25mm (US 3) needles.
1st row K to end.
2nd row K3, p to end.
3rd to 10th rows Rep 1st and 2nd rows 4 times more.
11th row K to end.
12th row K42(44:46:48:50), p to end.
13th and 14th rows As 11th and 12th rows.

These 14 rows form the st st with patt panel.
Cont in patt until front measures 16(19:22:25:28)cm/6 ¼(7 ½:8 ¾:
9 ¾:11)in from cast on edge, ending with a wrong side row.
Shape armhole
Next row Cast off 3(3:4:4:5) sts, patt to end. 55(59:62:66:69) sts.
Next row Patt to end.
Next row K2, skpo, patt to end.
Next row Patt to end.
Rep the last 2 rows 5(6:6:7:7) times. 49(52:55:58:61) sts.
Work straight until front measures 24(27:31:34:38)cm/9 ½(10 ½:
12 ¼:13 ¼:15)in from cast on edge, ending with a p row.
Shape neck
Next row Patt to last 29(31:33:35:37) sts, leave these sts on a holder.
Next row Patt to end.
Next row Patt to last 4 sts, k2 tog, k2.
Rep the last 2 rows 6 times more. 13(14:15:16:17) sts.
Cont straight until front measures same as back to shoulder,
ending at armhole edge.
Shape shoulder
Cast off 6(7:7:8:8) sts at beg of next row.
Work 1 row.
Cast off rem 7(7:8:8:9) sts.
With right side facing, slip centre 16(18:20:22:24) sts on a
holder, rejoin yarn to rem sts, patt to end.
Next row Patt to end.
Next row K2, skpo, k to end.
Rep the last 2 rows 6 times more. 6 sts.
Cont straight until front measures same as back to shoulder,
ending at front edge.
K 3 rows.
Cast off.

RIGHT FRONT

With 3mm (US 2) needles cast on 62(68:74:80:86) sts.
1st rib row P2, [k4, p2] to end.
2nd rib row K2, [p4, k2] to last 6 sts, p6.
Rep the last 2 rows 7 times more.
Next row Cast off 4(6:8:10:12) sts, using 3.25mm (US 3) needle, k to end - this counts as first patt row. 58(62:66:70:74) sts.
2nd row P to last 3 sts, k3.
3rd row K to end.
4th row P to last 3 sts, k3.
5th to 10th rows Rep 3rd and 4th rows 3 times more.
11th row K to end.
12th row P16(18:20:22:24), k to end.
13th and 14th rows As 11th and 12th rows.
These 14 rows form the st st with patt panel.
Cont in patt until front measures 16(19:22:25:28)cm/6 ¼ (7 ½:8 ¾: 9 ¾:11)in from cast on edge, ending with a right side row.
Shape armhole
Next row Cast off 3(3:4:4:5) sts, patt to end. 55(59:62:66:69) sts.
Next row K to last 4 sts, k2 tog, k2.
Next row Patt to end.
Rep the last 2 rows 5(6:6:7:7) times. 49(52:55:58:61) sts.
Work straight until front measures 24(27:31:34:38)cm/9 ½(10 ½: 12 ¼:13 ¼:15)in from cast on edge, ending with a p row.
Shape neck
Next row Patt 13 sts, turn and work on these sts. Leave rem sts on a holder.
Next row Patt to end.
Next row Patt to last 4 sts, k2 tog, k2.
Rep the last 2 rows 6 times more. 6 sts.
Cont straight until front measures same as back to shoulder, ending at neck edge.
K 3 rows.
Cast off.
With right side facing, slip centre 16(18:20:22:24) sts on a

holder, rejoin yarn to rem sts, patt to end.
Next row Patt to end.
Next row K2, skpo, patt to end.
Rep the last 2 rows 6 times more. 13(14:15:16:17) sts.
Cont straight until front measures same as back to shoulder, ending at armhole edge.
Shape shoulder
Cast off 6(7:7:8:8) sts at beg of next row.
Work 1 row.
Cast off rem 7(7:8:8:9) sts.

SLEEVES

With 3mm (US 2) needles cast on 41(44:44:47:47) sts.
1st rib row K2, [p1, k2] to end.
2nd rib row P2, [k1, p2] to end.
Rep the last 2 rows 7 times more.
Change to 3.25mm (US 3) needles.
Beg with a k row, cont in st st.
Work 2 rows.
Inc row K3, m1, k to last 3 sts, m1, k3.
Work 5 rows.
Rep the last 6 rows 6(7:9:11:13) times more, and then the inc row again. 57(62:66:73:77) sts.
Cont straight until sleeve measures 24(27:30:33:36)cm/9 ½(10 ½: 11 ¾:13:14 ¼)in from cast on edge, ending with a p row.
Shape sleeve top
Cast off 3(3:4:4:5) sts at beg of next 2 rows. 51(56:58:65:67) sts.
Next row K2, skpo, k to last 4 sts, k2 tog, k2.
Next row P to end.
Rep the last 2 rows 10(11:12:14:15) times. 29(32:32:35:35) sts.
Cast off 3 sts at beg of next 6(6:6:8:8) rows.
Cast off.

COLLAR

Join shoulder seams.

With right side facing, using 3mm (US 2) circular needle, pick up and k12(14:15:17:18) sts down left side of neck on right front, k16(18:20:22:24) across centre front, pick up and k12(14:14:16:16) sts up right side of neck, k30(32:34:36:38) across back neck, pick up and k12(14:14:16:16) sts down left side of neck on left front, k16(18:20:22:24) across centre front, pick up and k12(14:15:17:18) sts up right side of neck. 110(124:132:146:154) sts.

Next 2 rows Cast off 20(23:25:26:28) sts, k to end. 70(78:82:94:98) sts.

Next row K4, [p2, k2] to last 6 sts, p2, k4.

Next row K2, [p2, k2] to end.

These 2 rows form the rib with g-st edging.

Work a further 18(20:22:24:26) rows.

Cast off in patt.

TO MAKE UP

Join side and sleeve seams. Sew in sleeves. Sew on poppers placing two poppers along the ribbed hem and one on each side of the collar at shoulder, and the rest spaced evenly up the chosen front. Sew on buttons.

KALLE TANK TOP

SKILL LEVEL **Improving**

SIZES / MEASUREMENTS

To fit age	3-6	6-12	12-24	12-24	36-48	48-60	mths

ACTUAL GARMENT MEASUREMENTS

Chest	41	46	51	56	61	65	cm
	16	18	20	22	24	25½	in
Length to	25	27	30	33	37	41	cm
shoulder	10	10 ½	11 ¾	13	14 ½	16	in

MATERIALS

2(2:2:3:3:3) 50g/1 ¾oz balls of MillaMia Naturally Soft Merino in Midnight (101) (M).
Two balls of contrast colour Storm (102) (C).
Pair of 3mm (US 2) knitting needles.
Two long double pointed or shorter circular 3.25mm (US 3) knitting needles.

TENSION / GAUGE

25 sts and 34 rows to 10cm/4in square over st st using 3.25mm (US 3) needles.

HINTS AND TIPS

When you work in a single row stripe pattern and work flat (as opposed to in the round), you normally have to cut the yarn and re-join yarn for the new colour which leaves you with plenty of ends to sew in. However by using circular or long double pointed needles there is a technique you can use which allows you to avoid this, and this pattern is written to take advantage of this. This method applies only to flat knitting (not circular) and you achieve it as follows:

When the colour of the yarn you want to knit on the next row is not at the beginning of the next row (because it is still at the beginning of the previous row), rather than turning the work as you would usually, pull your work all the way to the other end of the needle from where you would normally have started – effectively you return to the beginning of the previous row. Then start working from there instead. For stocking stitch always knit on right side rows and purl on wrong side rows. Importantly this means that you will knit two consecutive right side rows and then two consecutive wrong side rows, rather than alternating every row.

ABBREVIATIONS

See page 9.

SUGGESTED ALTERNATIVE COLOURWAYS

Claret	Fawn		Moss	Snow		Midnight	Fawn
104	160		103	124		101	160

20 ½ (23 : 25 ½ : 28 : 30 ½ : 32 ½) cm
8 (9 :10 : 11 : 12 : 12 ¾) in

25 (27 : 30 : 33 : 37 : 41) cm
10 (10 ½ : 11 ¾ : 13 : 14 ½ : 16) in

BACK

With 3mm (US 2) needles and M, cast on 54(58:66:70:78:82) sts.
1st rib row K2, [p2, k2] to end.
2nd rib row P2, [k2, p2] to end.
Rep the last 2 rows 3(3:4:4:5:5) times more, inc 2 sts evenly across last row on **2nd, 4th and 6th sizes** only.
54(60:66:72:78:84) sts.
Change to 3.25mm (US 3) needles.
See Hints and Tips.
1st row Using M, k to end.
2nd row Return to beg of row, by sliding work along knitting needle. Using C, k to end.
3rd row Using M, p to end.
4th row Return to beg of row. Using C, p to end.
These 4 rows form the stripe patt.
Cont in patt until back measures 15(16:18:20:23:26)cm/ 6(6 ¼:7:8:9:10 ¼)in from cast on edge, ending with a 1st or 3rd row.
Shape armholes
Cast off 5 sts at beg of next 2 rows. 44(50:56:62:68:74) sts **.
Next row Patt 2, patt 2 tog, patt to last 4 sts, patt 2 tog, patt 2.
Next row Patt to end.
Rep the last 2 rows 2(3:4:5:6:7) times. 38(42:46:50:54:58) sts.
Cont in st st until back measures 25(27:30:33:37:41)cm/ 10(10 ½: 11 ¾:13:14 ½:16)in from cast on edge, ending with a 1st or 3rd row.
Shape shoulders
Cast off 7(8:9:10:11:12) sts at beg of next 2 rows.
Leave rem 24(26:28:30:32:34) sts on a holder.

FRONT

Work as given for back to **.
Shape front neck
Next row Patt 2, patt 2 tog, patt 13(16:19:22:25:28), patt 2 tog, patt 2, turn and work on these sts for first side of front neck.
Next row Patt to end.
Next row Patt 2, patt 2 tog, patt to last 4 sts, patt 2 tog, patt 2.
Rep the last 2 rows 2(3:4:5:6:7) times. 13(14:15:16:17:18) sts.
Keeping armhole edge straight cont to dec at neck edge on every foll 4th row until 7(8:9:10:11:12) sts rem.
Cont straight until front measures same as back to shoulder, ending at armhole edge.
Shape shoulder
Cast off.
Return to sts for second side of front neck, slip centre 2 sts onto a safety pin, join on yarn to rem sts.
Next row Patt 2, patt 2 tog, patt to last 4 sts, patt 2 tog, patt 2.
Next row Patt to end.
Next row Patt 2, patt 2 tog, patt to last 4 sts, patt 2 tog, patt 2.
Rep the last 2 rows 2(3:4:5:6:7) times. 13(14:15:16:17:18) sts.
Keeping armhole edge straight cont to dec at neck edge on every foll 4th row until 7(8:9:10:11:12) sts rem.
Cont straight until front measures same as back to shoulder, ending at armhole edge.
Shape shoulder
Cast off.

NECKBAND

Join right shoulder seam.
With right side facing, using 3mm (US 2) needles and M, pick up and k36(38:40:44:46:48) sts evenly down left side of front neck, k2 from safety pin, pick up and k36(36:40:42:46:46) sts evenly up right side of front neck, k24(26:28:30:32:34) sts from back neck holder. 98(102:110:118:126:130) sts.
1st, 3rd, 4th and 6th sizes only
1st row P2, [k2, p2] to end.
2nd and 5th sizes only
1st row K2, [p2, k2] to end.
All sizes
This row sets the rib patt.
2nd row Rib 35(37:39:43:45:47), k2 tog, skpo, rib to end.
3rd row Rib to end.
4th row Rib 34(36:38:42:44:46), k2 tog, skpo, rib to end.
5th row Rib to end.
6th row Cast off in rib, dec on this row as before.

ARMBANDS

Join left shoulder seam and neckband.
With right side facing, using 3mm (US 2) needles and M, pick up and k78(82:86:94:98:102) sts evenly around armhole edge.
1st row P2, [k2, p2] to end.
2nd row K2, [p2, k2] to end.
These 2 rows set the rib patt.
Work a further 3 rows.
Cast off in rib.

TO MAKE UP

Join side and armband seams.

GUSTAV
HAT & SCARF
INGA
WRIST WARMERS

From left to right: **Gustav Hat & Scarf** in Plum (162) and Fawn (160) and **Gustav Hat & Scarf** in Seaside (161) and Snow (124) pattern on page 94 and **Inga Wrist Warmers** in Seaside (161) and Snow (124) pattern on page 98

GUSTAV HAT & SCARF

SKILL LEVEL **Scarf – Beginner / Hat – Improving**

SIZES / MEASUREMENTS

To fit age   2-5 yr old, one size

ACTUAL MEASUREMENTS

Scarf   16cm/6 ¼in wide by 130cm/51in long
Hat   One size to fit 2-5 years

MATERIALS

Scarf Three 50g/1 ¾oz balls of MillaMia Naturally Soft Merino in Plum (162) (M).
One ball in Fawn (160) (C).
Pair of 3.25mm (US 3) knitting needles.
Hat Two 50g/1 ¾oz balls of MillaMia Naturally Soft Merino in Plum (162) (M).
One ball in Fawn (160) (C).
Pair of 3.25mm (US 3) knitting needles.
Circular 3.25mm (US 3) knitting needle.

TENSION / GAUGE

25 sts and 34 rows to 10cm/4in over st st using 3.25mm (US 3) needles.

HINTS AND TIPS

Ever useful – the earflaps on the Gustav Hat keep them warm and snuggly and the built in pockets on the scarf will protect their hands from a chill if you forget their gloves. Make sure you block the pockets flat before you attach them to the scarf. Use mattress stich to attach the pockets to create a seamless finish.

ABBREVIATIONS

See page 9.

SUGGESTED ALTERNATIVE COLOURWAYS

Seaside 161   Snow 124   Fuchsia 143   Daisy Yellow 142   Petal 122   Putty Grey 121   Forget me not 120   Snow 102

16 cm / 6 ¼ in

130 cm / 51 in

SCARF

With 3.25mm (US 3) needles and M cast on 46 sts.
1st row K2, [p2, k2] to end.
2nd row P2, [k2, p2] to end.
These 2 rows form the rib.
Work a further 8 rows C, 2 rows M in rib.
Cut off C.
Cont in M.
1st row (right side) P1, [k1, p1] twice, k to last 5 sts, [p1, k1] twice, p1.
2nd row [P1, k1] twice, p to last 4 sts, [k1, p1] twice.
Rep the last 2 rows until scarf measures 127cm/50in long, ending with a wrong side row.
Cont in rib as given at beginning, work 2 rows M, 8 rows C, 2 rows M.
Using M cast off.

POCKETS (make 2)

With 3.25mm (US 3) needles and C cast on 30 sts.
Beg with a k row cont in st st and stripes of [2 rows C, 4 rows M] 6 times, inc 2 sts across last row.
1st rib row Using M, k3, [p2, k2] to last 5 sts, p2, k3.
2nd rib row Using M, p3, [k2, p2] to last 5 sts, k2, p3.
These 2 rows form the rib.
Work a further 8 rows C and 2 rows M.
Using M cast off in rib.

MAKE UP

Sew on pockets centrally above rib.

HAT

EAR FLAPS (make 2)

With 3.25mm (US 3) needles and M cast on 6 sts.
Next row P to end.
Cont in stripes of 2 rows C and 4 rows M.
Next row K1, m1, k to last st, m1, k1.
Next row P1, m1p, p to last st, m1p, p1.
Rep the last 2 rows once more. 14 sts.
Next row K2, m1, k to last 2 sts, m1, k2.
Next row P to end.
Rep the last 2 rows 4 times more. 24 sts.
Next row K to end.
Next row P to end.
Rep the last 2 rows 6 times more.
Leave these sts on a holder.

MAIN PART

With a spare 3.25mm (US 3) needle and M, cast on 13 sts, break off yarn then onto same needle cast on another 31 sts, break off yarn.

With 3.25mm (US 3) needles and M, cast on 13 sts, k these 13 sts, then k across 24 sts of first ear flap, k31 sts from spare needle, then k across 24 sts of second ear flap, then k13 sts from spare needle. 105 sts.

Next row P to end.

Cont in st st and stripes of 2 rows C and 4 rows M until main part measures 14cm/5 ½in from cast on edge, ending with a p row.

Dec row K1, [skpo, k6] to end. 92 sts.

P 1 row.

Dec row K1, [skpo, k5] to end. 79 sts.

P 1 row.

Dec row K1, [skpo, k4] to end. 66 sts.

P 1 row.

Dec row K1, [skpo, k3] to end. 53 sts.

P 1 row.

Dec row K1, [skpo, k2] to end. 40 sts.

P 1 row.

Dec row K1, [skpo, k1] to end. 27 sts.

P 1 row.

Dec row K1, [skpo] to end. 14 sts.

P 1 row.

Dec row [Skpo] to end. 7 sts.

P 1 row.

Cut off yarn, thread through rem sts, pull up and secure.

EDGING

With right side facing, using 3.25mm (US 3) circular needle and M pick up and k13 sts along cast on edge of back, * 13 sts along straight edge of earflap, 29 sts around shaped edge of earflap, 13 sts along straight edge of earflap *, 30 sts along cast on edge; rep from * to * once more, 13 sts along cast on edge. 166 sts.

Work backwards and forwards in rows.

1st row P2, [k2, p2] to end.

2nd row K2, [p2, k2] to end.

Rep the last 2 rows once more, and then the first row again.

Cast off in rib.

TIES (make 2)

With 3.25mm (US 3) needles and M, cast on 7 sts.

1st row K2, p1, k1, p1, k2.

2nd row K1, [p1, k1] 3 times.

Rep the last 2 rows until tie measures 30cm/12in from cast on edge.

Cast off in rib.

MAKE UP

Join back and edging seam. Sew one tie to each earflap.

INGA WRISTWARMERS

SKILL LEVEL **Beginner**

SIZES /MEASUREMENTS

To fit age	Toddler	Child

ACTUAL MEASUREMENTS

Length	19	22	cm
	7 ½	8 ¾	in
Width	7	8	cm
	2 ¾	3	in

MATERIALS

1(2) 50g/1 ¾oz ball(s) of MillaMia Naturally Soft Merino in Fuchsia (143) (M).
One ball of contrast Daisy Yellow (142) (C).
Pair each of 3mm (US 2) and 3.25mm (US 3) knitting needles.

TENSION / GAUGE

25 sts and 34 rows to 10cm/4in square over st st using 3.25mm(US 3) needles.

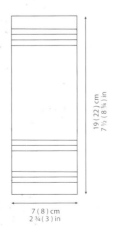

7 (8) cm
2 ¾ (3) in

19 (22) cm
7 ½ (8 ¾) in

HINTS AND TIPS

The perfect present - so quick and so easy. You can make these in a couple of evenings.

ABBREVIATIONS

See page 9.

SUGGESTED ALTERNATIVE COLOURWAYS

Seaside	Snow		Petal	Putty Grey		Plum	Fawn
161	124		122	121		162	160

TO MAKE

With 3.25mm (US 3) needles and M cast on 37(42) sts.
1st row (right side) P2, [k3, p2] to end.
2nd row K2, [p3, k2] to end.
These 2 rows form the rib.
Work a further 4 rows M, 2 rows C, 2 rows M, 8 rows C, 2 rows M, 2 rows C, 4 rows M.
Beg with a k row cont in M and st st.
Work 22 (32) rows.
Now work in rib patt.
Work 4 rows M, 2 rows C, 2 rows M, 2 rows C, 6 rows M.
Cast off in rib.

TO MAKE UP

Join seam, leaving a 3cm/1 ¼in gap for thumb starting 13(16)cm/5 ¼(6¼)in from the cast on edge.

HANNA
CARDIGAN
MADELEINE
DRESS

From left to right: **Hanna Cardigan** in Daisy Yellow (142), Peacock (144) and Fuchsia (143) pattern on page 102 and **Madeleine Dress** in Fuchsia (143) and Peacock (144) pattern on page 108

HANNA CARDIGAN

SKILL LEVEL **Beginner / Improving**

SIZES / MEASUREMENTS

To fit age	1-2	2-3	3-4	4-5	5-6	years

ACTUAL GARMENT MEASUREMENTS

Chest	58	62	68	72	76	cm
	23	24 ½	27	28 ½	30	in
Length to shoulder	28	32	36	40	44	cm
	11	12 ½	14 ¼	15 ¾	17 ½	in
Sleeve length	21	24	26	28	31	cm
	8 ¼	9 ½	10 ¼	11	12 ¼	in

MATERIALS

2(2:2:3:3) 50g/1 ¾oz balls of MillaMia Naturally Soft Merino in each of Daisy Yellow (142) (A), Peacock (144) (B) and Fuchsia (143) (C).
Pair each of 3mm (US 2) and 3.25mm (US 3) knitting needles.
Circular 3mm (US 2) knitting needle.
3(4:4:5:5) small poppers.

TENSION / GAUGE

25 sts and 34 rows to 10cm/4in square over st st using 3.25mm (US 3) needles.

HINTS AND TIPS

A fun vibrant cardigan that would also look elegant and refined in more muted colours. If you are new to short row shaping when it comes to making the bows, why not look on the internet for some advice on 'garter stitch short row shaping' to help prevent any holes in your bows.

ABBREVIATIONS

See page 9.

SUGGESTED ALTERNATIVE COLOURWAYS

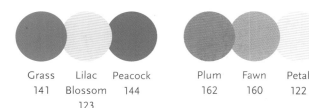

Grass 141   Lilac Blossom 123   Peacock 144   Plum 162   Fawn 160   Petal 122

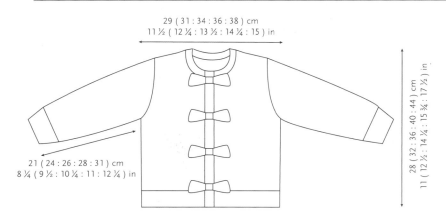

29 (31 : 34 : 36 : 38) cm
11 ½ (12 ¼ : 13 ½ : 14 ¼ : 15) in

21 (24 : 26 : 28 : 31) cm
8 ¼ (9 ½ : 10 ¼ : 11 : 12 ¼) in

28 (32 : 36 : 40 : 44) cm
11 (12 ½ : 14 ¼ : 15 ¾ : 17 ½) in

STRIPE SEQUENCE FOR BACK AND FRONTS

12(15:17:20:22) rows B, 12(15:17:20:22) rows C,
24(30:34:40:44) rows B, then cont in C.

BACK

With 3mm (US 2) needles and A cast on 74(80:86:92:98) sts.
1st rib row K2, [p1, k2] to end.
2nd rib row P2, [k1, p2] to end.
Rep the last 2 rows 7 times more.
Cut off A.
Change to 3.25mm (US 3) needles.
Beg with a k row, cont in st st and stripe sequence until back measures 16(19:22:25:28)cm/6 ¼(7 ½:8 ¾:9 ¾:11)in from cast on edge, ending with a p row.
Shape armholes
Cast off 3(3:4:4:5) sts at beg of next 2 rows.
68(74:78:84:88) sts.
Next row K2, skpo, k to last 4 sts, k2 tog, k2.
Next row P to end.
Rep the last 2 rows 5(6:6:7:7) times. 56(60:64:68:72) sts.
Cont in st st until back measures 28(32:36:40:44)cm/11(12 ½:14 ¼:15 ¾:17 ½)in from cast on edge, ending with a p row.
Shape shoulders
Cast off 6(7:7:8:8) sts at beg of next 2 rows and 7(7:8:8:9) sts at beg of foll 2 rows.
Leave rem 30(32:34:36:38) sts on a holder.

LEFT FRONT

With 3mm (US 2) needles and A cast on 33(36:39:42:45) sts.
1st rib row [K2, p1] to end.
2nd rib row [K1, p2] to end.
Rep the last 2 rows 7 times more.
Cut off A.
Change to 3.25mm (US 3) needles.
Beg with a k row, cont in st st and stripe sequence until left front measures 16(19:22:25:28)cm/6 ¼(7 ½:8 ¾:9 ¾:11)in from cast on edge, ending with a p row.
Shape armhole
Next row Cast off 3(3:4:4:5) sts, k to end. 30(33:35:38:40) sts.
Next row P to end.
Next row K2, skpo, k to end.
Next row P to end.
Rep the last 2 rows 5(6:6:7:7) times. 24(26:28:30:32) sts.
Work straight until front measures 24(27:31:34:38)cm/9 ½(10 ½:12 ¼:13 ¼:15)in from cast on edge, ending with a p row.
Shape neck
Next row K to last 8(8:9:9:10) sts, leave these sts on a holder.
Next row P to end.
Next row K to last 4 sts, k2 tog, k2.
Rep the last 2 rows until 13(14:15:16:17) sts rem.
Cont straight until front measures same as back to shoulder, ending at armhole edge.
Shape shoulder
Cast off 6(7:7:8:8) sts at beg of next row.
Work 1 row.
Cast off rem 7(7:8:8:9) sts.

RIGHT FRONT

With 3mm (US 2) needles and A cast on 33(36:39:42:45) sts.
1st rib row [P1, k2] to end.
2nd rib row [P2, k1] to end.
Rep the last 2 rows 7 times more.
Cut off A.
Change to 3.25mm (US 3) needles.
Beg with a k row, cont in st st and stripe sequence until right front measures 16(19:22:25:28)cm/6 ¼ (7 ½:8 ¾:9 ¾:11)in from cast on edge, ending with a k row.
Shape armhole
Next row Cast off 3(3:4:4:5) sts, p to end. 30(33:35:38:40) sts.
Next row K to last 4 sts, k2 tog, k2.
Next row P to end.
Rep the last 2 rows 5(6:6:7:7) times. 24(26:28:30:32) sts.
Work straight until front measures 24(27:31:34:38)cm/9 ½(10 ½: 12 ¼:13 ¼:15)in from cast on edge, ending with a p row.
Shape neck
Next row K8(8:9:9:10) sts, leave these sts on a holder, k to end.
Next row P to end.
Next row K2, skpo, k to end.
Rep the last 2 rows until 13(14:15:16:17) sts rem.
Cont straight until front measures same as back to shoulder, ending at armhole edge.
Shape shoulder
Cast off 6(7:7:8:8) sts at beg of next row.
Work 1 row.
Cast off rem 7(7:8:8:9) sts.

STRIPE SEQUENCE FOR SLEEVES

Make a note of how many rows are worked in B in armhole of front and back pieces.
20(20:20:20:20) rows B, 8(10:10:12:14) rows C, 14(15:15:16:17) rows A, approx 24(30:34:40:44) rows B, then cont in C.

SLEEVES

With 3mm (US 2) needles and A cast on 41(44:47:53:56) sts.
1st rib row K2, [p1, k2] to end.
2nd rib row P2, [k1, p2] to end.
Rep the last 2 rows 7 times more.
Cut off A.
Change to 3.25mm (US 3) needles.
Beg with a k row, cont in st st and stripe sequence.
Work 2 rows.
Inc row K3, m1, k to last 3 sts, m1, k3.
Work 5 rows.
Rep the last 6 rows 6(7:8:9:10) times more, and then the inc row again. 57(62:67:75:80) sts.
Cont straight until sleeve measures 21(24:26:28:31)cm/8 ¼ (9 ½: 10 ¼:11:12 ¼)in from cast on edge, ending with a p row.
Shape sleeve top
Note: when same number of rows have been worked in B as in armhole shaping, cont in C.
Cast off 3(3:4:4:5) sts at beg of next 2 rows. 51(56:59:67:70) sts.
Next row K2, skpo, k to last 4 sts, k2 tog, k2.
Next row P to end.
Rep the last 2 rows 10(11:12:14:15) times. 29(32:33:37:38) sts.
Cast off 3 sts at beg of next 6(6:6:8:8) rows.
Cast off.

NECKBAND

Join shoulder seams.
With right side facing, 3mm (US 2) needles and A, slip 8(8:9:9:10) sts from right front neck holder onto a needle, pick up and k12(12:15:15:18) sts up right front neck, k30(32:34:36:38) sts from back neck holder, pick up and k12(13:15:16:18) sts down left front neck, k8(8:9:9:10) sts from left front holder. 70(73:82:85:94) sts.
1st rib row K1, [p2, k1] to end.
2nd rib row P1, [k2, p1] to end.
Rep the last 2 rows twice more, and then the first row again.
Cast off in rib.

LEFT FRONT BAND

With right side facing, 3mm (US 2) needles and A, pick up and k61(70:76:85:91) sts down left front edge.
1st rib row K1, [p2, k1] to end.
2nd rib row P1, [k2, p1] to end.
Rep the last 2 rows twice more, and then the first row again.
Cast off in rib.

RIGHT FRONT BAND

With right side facing, 3mm (US 2) needles and A, pick up and k61(70:76:85:91) sts up right front edge.
1st rib row K1, [p2, k1] to end.
2nd rib row P1, [k2, p1] to end.
Rep the last 2 rows twice more, and then the first row again.
Cast off in rib.

BOW (make 3(4:4:5:5))

See Hints and Tips.
With 3mm (US 2) needles and A cast on 21 sts.
1st row K to end.
2nd and 3rd rows K8, turn, k to end.
Rep the last 3 rows 5 times more.
Cast off.

TO MAKE UP

Join side and sleeve seams. Sew in sleeves. Sew on bows with poppers behind to fasten.

MADELEINE DRESS

SKILL LEVEL Beginner / Improving

SIZES / MEASUREMENTS

To fit age	2-3	3-4	4-5	5-6	6-7	years

ACTUAL GARMENT MEASUREMENTS

Chest	56	61	66	70	75	cm
	22	24	26	27 ½	29 ½	in
Length to	50	56	62	68	74	cm
shoulder	19 ¾	22	24 ½	26 ¾	29	in

MATERIALS

4(5:6:6:7) 50g/1 ¾oz balls of MillaMia Naturally Soft Merino in Putty Grey (121) (M).
One ball of Fuchsia (143) (C).
Pair each of 3mm (US 2) and 3.25mm (US 3) needles.

TENSION/ GAUGE

25 sts and 34 rows to 10cm/4in square over st st using 3.25mm (US 3) needles.

HINTS AND TIPS

Press the bow flat before you attach it. If you are new to short row shaping when it comes to making the bows, why not look on the internet for some advice on 'garter stitch short row shaping' to help prevent any holes in your bows. As ever colour has such an impact on this design – veer from the fun bright combinations we have shown to a more traditional maritime combination of Midnight (101) and Snow (124).

ABBREVIATIONS

See page 9.

SUGGESTED ALTERNATIVE COLOURWAYS

Fuchsia	Peacock	Midnight	Snow	Petal	Moss
143	144	101	124	122	103

28 (30 ½ : 33 : 35 : 37 ½) cm
11 (12 : 13 : 13 ¾ : 14 ¾) in

50 (56 : 62 : 68 : 74) cm
19 ¾ (22 : 24 ½ : 26 ¾ : 29) in

BACK

With 3mm (US 2) needles and C cast on 92(98:104:110:116) sts.
K 7 rows.
Cut off C.
Change to 3.25mm (US 3) needles.
Join on M.
Beg with a k row cont in st st.
Work 10(12:14:16:18) rows.
Dec row K4, skpo, k to last 6 sts, k2 tog, k4.
Work 9(11:13:15:17) rows.
Rep the last 10(12:14:16:18) rows 8 times more, and then the dec row again. 72(78:84:90:96) sts.
Work 1 row.
Work 4 rows C, 8 rows M and 4 rows C.
Cont in st st and M only until back measures 40(45:50:55:60)cm/ 15 ¾(17 ¾:19 ¾:21 ¾:23 ¾)in from cast on edge, ending with a wrong side row.
Mark each end of last row with a coloured thread to denote beg of armhole shaping **.
Shape armholes
Next row K2, m1, k to last 2 sts, m1, k2.
Work 3 rows.
Rep the last 4 rows 6(7:8:9:10) times more.
86(94:102:110:118) sts.
Shape back neck
Next row K30(33:36:39:42), turn and work on these sts.
Dec one st at neck edge on next 4 rows. 26(29:32:35:38) sts.
Work 1 row.
Shape shoulder
Cast off 5(5:6:6:7) sts at the beg of next and 2 foll right side rows.
Work 1 row.
Cast off 5(7:7:8:8) sts at beg of next row.
Work 1 row.
Cast off rem 6(7:7:9:9) sts.
With right side facing slip centre 26(28:30:32:34) sts on a holder, rejoin yarn to rem sts, k to end.
Dec one st at neck edge on next 4 rows. 26(29:32:35:38) sts.
Work 2 rows.

Shape shoulder
Cast off 5(5:6:6:7) sts at the beg of next and 2 foll wrong side rows.
Work 1 row.
Cast off 5(7:7:8:8) sts at beg of next row.
Work 1 row.
Cast off rem 6(7:7:9:9) sts.

FRONT

Work as given for back to **.
Shape armholes
Next row K2, m1, k to last 2 sts, m1, k2.
Work 3 rows.
Rep the last 4 rows 2(3:4:5:6) times more. 78(86:94:102:110) sts.
Shape back neck
Next row K2, m1, k24(27:30:33:36), k2 tog, k2, turn and work on these sts.
Next row P to end.
Next row K to last 4 sts, k2 tog, k2.
Next row P to end.
Next row K2, m1, k to last 4 sts, k2 tog, k2.
Rep the last 4 rows twice more. 27(30:33:36:39) sts.
Next row P to end.
Next row K to last 4 sts, k2 tog, k2. 26(29:32:35:38) sts.
Work 7 rows.
Shape shoulder
Cast off 5(5:6:6:7) sts at the beg of next and 2 foll right side rows.
Work 1 row.
Cast off 5(7:7:8:8) sts at beg of next row.
Work 1 row.
Cast off rem 6(7:7:9:9) sts.
With right side facing slip centre 18(20:22:24:26) sts on a holder, rejoin yarn to rem sts, k2, skpo, k to last 2 sts, m1, k2.
Next row P to end.
Next row K2, skpo, k to end.
Next row P to end.
Next row K2, skpo, k to last 2 sts, m1, k2.
Rep the last 4 rows twice more. 27(30:33:36:39) sts.

Next row P to end.
Next row K2, skpo, k to end. 26(29:32:35:38) sts.
Work 8 rows.
Shape shoulder
Cast off 5(5:6:6:7) sts at the beg of next and 2 foll wrong side rows.
Work 1 row.
Cast off 5(7:7:8:8) sts at beg of next row.
Work 1 row.
Cast off rem 6(7:7:9:9) sts.

NECKBAND

Join right shoulder seam.
With 3mm (US 2) needles and C pick up and k20 sts down left side of front neck, k18(20:22:24:26) sts on front neck holder, pick up and k20 sts up right side of front neck, 7 sts down right side of back neck, k26(28:30:32:34) sts on back neck holder, pick up and k7 sts up left side of back neck. 98(102:106:110:114) sts.
1st row K to end.
2nd row K18, k2 tog, skpo, k14(16:18:20:22), k2 tog, skpo, k to end.
3rd row K to end.
4th row K17, k2 tog, skpo, k12(14:16:18:20), k2 tog, skpo, k to end.
5th row K to end.
6th row K16, k2 tog, skpo, k10(12:14:16:18), k2 tog, skpo, k to end.
Cast off.

ARMBANDS

Join left shoulder and neckband seam.
With 3mm (US 2) needles and C pick up and k61(67:73:79:85) sts evenly round armhole edge between markers.
K 6 rows.
Cast off.

BOW

See Hints and Tips.
With 3mm (US 2) needles and M cast on 21 sts.
1st row K to end.
2nd and 3rd rows K12, turn, k to end.
Rep the last 3 rows 9 times more.
Cast off.

TO MAKE UP

Join side seams and armband seams. Sew on bow.

YARN COLOURS

Midnight
101

Storm
102

Moss
103

Claret
104

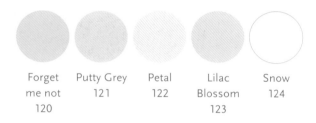

Forget
me not
120

Putty Grey
121

Petal
122

Lilac
Blossom
123

Snow
124

Scarlet
140

Grass
141

Daisy
Yellow
142

Fuchsia
143

Peacock
144

Fawn
160

Seaside
161

Plum
162

NOTES

INDEX

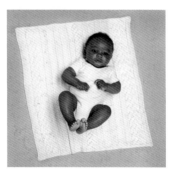

MAX BABYGROW
page 62

MATTIAS CARDIGAN
page 68

OLIVER SLEEPING BAG
page 72

LARS JUMPER
page 76

KASPER JACKET
page 82

KALLE TANK TOP
page 88

GUSTAV HAT & SCARF
AND INGA WRIST WARMERS
page 94 and page 98

HANNA CARDIGAN
page 102

MADELEINE DRESS
page 108

FROM MILLAMIA

It is hard to believe that we are now publishing our fourth book of patterns for babies and children! The last few years have sped by since our launch with the publication of The Close Knit Gang. We swiftly followed with Bright Young Things and then waited to see how knitters would react.

We could not have asked for a better reception – the combination of the elegant, vintage-inspired styles in The Close Knit Gang and the colourful, quirky patterns in Bright Young Things seemed to resonate with many of you and we were so delighted to get such positive feedback – both verbally at the various knitting shows we have done in the UK and abroad, but also by email and other modern digital media. We particularly love the interaction we have with many of you on our Facebook page and our Ravelry group. There is nothing more rewarding than seeing finished knitted MillaMia designs being modelled by adorable kids all across the world in the photos that you post!

Following on from the success of the first two books we had a bit of trepidation. Would we be able to live up to the positive response we had been lucky enough to earn already? The funny thing is that as soon as we saw our third book Wonderland laid out in its pre-publication format, we felt confident about it. We knew that we had listened to your feedback with requests for more patterns for boys and also grading to older sizes. We also knew from the response to the samples when we had previewed them at shows that there were lots of so-called 'killer' items – the patterns that people cannot wait to knit! And our confidence proved deserved - Wonderland sold out of its first print run faster than either of our previous books.

We are learning all the time – so hopefully our books will be getting better and better too. We do strive to continually improve - whether this be in the yarn estimates given, the hints and tips we provide, through to the shaping. We hope you will see the benefits of this learning process in our fourth collection.

Little Rascals was one of the most creative photoshoots we have ever done. We do pride ourselves on giving a lot of thought to how we present our designs – whether that is in different sizes, different colourways or even on different gender models, but in this case we really went to town working with a very talented illustrator, Aurelie Bouget for the stunning backdrops you can see in the book. Despite the time pressure we were under at the time of the shoot for this book, we have to say that we could not have been more pleased with the end result and the scenes that Aurelie came up with. As a result of this – and working with our beloved photographer Emma Noren who has been with us from the start – the photoshoot was instantly rewarding despite the frenetic pace and ambitious schedule we had.

We are so excited to share these images and designs with you and are delighted to now present you with the fourth MillaMia Modern Baby and Childrens knitting pattern collection: Little Rascals. We hope you enjoy it!

With best wishes,

Katarina and Helena Rosén
katarina@millamia.com or helena@millamia.com